Soaring in the Prophetic

Bible Study

Berta Robison

His
PUBLISHING

COVER GRAPHICS BY BERTA ROBISON
IDAHO SUNSET PROVIDED BY GOD

ABOUT THE COVER:
REVELATION 4:1 "AFTER THIS I LOOKED, AND THERE BEFORE ME WAS A DOOR STANDING OPEN IN HEAVEN. AND THE VOICE I HAD FIRST HEARD SPEAKING TO ME LIKE A TRUMPET SAID, "COME UP HERE, AND I WILL SHOW YOU WHAT MUST TAKE PLACE AFTER THIS."

GOD IS ALWAYS CALLING HIS PEOPLE TO 'COME UP' HIGHER IN ORDER TO 'LET US IN ON HIS SECRETS.' ON THE COVER, WE SEE AN EAGLE 'SOARING OVER' CURRENT HAPPENINGS, CURRENT CIRCUMSTANCES, OVER THE 'STATUS QUO.' IN ORDER TO HAVE HIS PERSPECTIVE ON 'WHAT IS' AND 'WHAT IS TO COME' WE TOO MUST ALSO SOAR, IN THE PROPHETIC. –GARY BITTNER

Published by Hebrews 1:8 Publishing
ISBN-13:978-0615798561 (Hebrews 1:8 Publishing)
ISBN-10:061579856X

Dedication

I dedicate this book to my family. And, to all my friends—new and old—who have loved me and walked with me on the mountain heights and through the valley's depths. You are treasured.

And, to those venturous souls who were a part of our *Soaring in the Prophetic* small groups—what fun we had!

Table of Contents

• •

Chapter 4

Chapter 5

Chapter 6

Appendix A

Notes

Forewords

◆ ◆

The apostle Paul said that apart from love, the best gift is prophecy. In my understanding, it's because of God's desire to commune with His people. He has always been speaking and wants us to listen. Looking back on years of ministry and serving the body of Christ, I can say apart from love, I agree with Paul whole-heartedly. There is nothing like an on time, in time word of encouragement, comfort, or exhortation to build up the saints in identity and purpose. That's true whether it comes from anointed preaching or a personal anointed word given with love and humility.

I have known Berta Robison and her husband George for nearly 20 years now. They both have a passion for God's word and to see the saints grow up into Christ. They are solid folks who walk in love and integrity with others. They love the Church, the lost, and their family. Why do I mention that? The spirit of prophecy is the testimony of Jesus. Our testimony is also important to give authority and confidence in the words we speak. When they speak, I listen.

This manual on the prophetic is really well laid out and has the right heart and content to help both those who are just learning about prophecy and inspire those who have a history with the prophetic. It can be used as a tool for training or just enjoyed for personal growth.

I highly recommend it for either purpose. Thank you, Berta, for your love for the church, and your passion to hear the voice of God. This manual is a credit and testimony to your years of love and labor in the Lord.

—Denny Cline, Senior Leader at Jesus Pursuit Church in Albany, OR

• •

I have known Berta Robison for approximately 30 years and she is one the most passionate lovers of Jesus I have ever met. From her first days walking in the Spirit, she has had a sincere and burning desire for a 'pure word' from the Lord for her generation and has been faithful to 'deliver' as the Holy Spirit has prompted her. *Soaring in the Prophetic* is not Berta's theory, it is an exploration of the prophetic ministry based on exhaustive study of scripture, her own experience, and the experiences of others that have taught and mentored her over the years.

In *Soaring in the Prophetic,* Berta has provided an excellent study on the prophetic gift and ministry. God's desire has always been that by His Spirit we continue to speak a 'now' word to the 'now' generation. In this study, you will find an exposition on 'what' the prophetic ministry is, how it is to operate today through individuals, how it is to operate in corporate gatherings of the saints, practical helps to develop your prophetic gift and much more.

There is a desperate need for the prophetic ministry today, 'now.' God has never stopped speaking to His people and His desire is that His people speak for Him 'now.' We are in desperate times 'now.' And, God has a 'now' word for us to bring to our generation, 'now.' In 1 Chronicles 12:32 we read this: "... from Issachar, men who understood the times and knew what Israel should do." We need such people today.

One of the greatest benefits of the prophetic ministry is that it helps us receive and maintain a 'heavenly perspective' on 'earthly times and situations.' Without an active operation of the prophetic ministry, we often times 'see' something but 'read' it wrong. For example, the colors of sunrise and sunset are the same. If you see the colors but have the wrong perspective you may 'perceive' that darkness is falling on that dream, that vision, that promise and therefore it is 'time to give up' but in actuality it may be sunrise and a new day may be dawning on that dream, that vision, that promise and therefore it is 'time to go on!'

Read, study, be encouraged, and then, soar.

God bless,

Gary Bittner

Preface

◆ ◆

I F YOU HAVE THIS STUDY IN YOUR HAND, I assume you have some interest in the prophetic. Every Christian can and should be used in the prophetic gifts as the Apostle Paul makes clear in 1 Corinthian 14:5, "I would like every one of you to speak in tongues, but I would rather have you prophesy. He who prophesies is greater than one who speaks in tongues, unless he interprets, so that the church may be edified." By "the prophetic," I mean, in very basic terms, any gift from God where a person first hears from God and then does something with what they hear. The prophetic includes gifts such as words of knowledge, encouragements, prophetic intercessions, prophecies, exhortations, and words of wisdom.

Soaring in the Prophetic is an effective equipping tool in diverse settings whether for personal Bible study, group-equipping classes, small groups, or one-on-one discipling. From the one just starting to wade into the waters of the prophetic and to those with years of experience hearing God, *Soaring* will help anyone who has a heart to grow and learn. As we studying *Soaring,* we will learn to more effectively and more accurately manifest the heart of God as we communicate what we hear. *Soaring* will also help us to recognize the source of the struggles we face as we press into the gifts of the Spirit and how to overcome.

As I look back over my own journey, I understand how important input from other more seasoned prophetic people would have been. I am sure it would have spared me many of my own struggles. Hearing God is just the first step. What we do with what we hear is equally important. Let us determine to be excellent not only hearing God, but also in displaying the heart of God as we communicate the prophetic gifts to others.

God was visiting His people. It was the mid-1990s and we were in the middle of what some have called the *Renewal of the 1990s.* I had been a Christian and involved in the prophetic flow of Christianity since early 1980. General teaching had given me a good foundation in the gifts of the Spirit (for which I am grateful) however, my only mentoring was a few prophetic persons' examples. I had zeal, I made mistakes (a lot of them), but I kept pressing into the prophetic gifts often limping as I went. Now it was mid-1990s, nearly a decade and a half since I had received Jesus Christ; I was deep in the prophetic and in the midst of Holy

Spirit visitation. It was in these days God gave me revelation about 1 Corinthians 13—The Heart of the Prophetic which is the core of this book.

Chapter 2, The Heart of the Prophetic, is a study of the prophetic gifts in view of 1 Corinthians 13 and came as a revelation from the Holy Spirit, an "ah hah!" moment if you will. Penning it into an essay, I then shared it with my pastor. We agreed it seemed best to turn *Soaring in the Prophetic* into a Bible study for small group settings. Together with my husband, we led multiple small groups through *Soaring in the Prophetic*. I divided the material into 13 weekly studies so the small group had a beginning and an end, 14 weeks in all. We asked people to sign up for the small group and kept the size to about 12 people in each session. I asked two commitments from the beginning: first that people would be faithful to the meetings since others were waiting to take the class and secondly, if they did not work on their homework, not contribute during the discussion.

The small group had great dynamics. We began with about 45 minutes of worship using CDs. I would fast until God gave me the song list and then I would create a play list so we could have uninterrupted worship. During worship, people would end up face down on the floor nearly every week, as the presence of the Lord would manifest.

At the beginning of each term, all the names were put in a pot with weekly drawings of either an individual or a couple. During the following week, the group would target pray for those who were drawn. When we met for the next study, "the chosen" would get the hot seat, which was a chair placed in the middle of the room. We would lay hands on them, pray, and prophesy as the Holy Spirit led. All this was recorded so what was said could be remembered. Feedback would also be given to those who prophesied.

Week 14 was the finale. One of the senior pastoral leaders would join us for the last meeting of the term in order to commission the graduates into prophetic ministry in the church. The leader would go over the expectations senior leaders had: the protocol and anything else, which was on their heart for the night. This gave the graduates confidence as they were released to operate in the gifts of the Spirit in the church. They would know what to do if they had a word from the Lord. In addition, it helped them get to know the leader better. The leader would lay hands on each one and bless them. It was great fun!

Whatever format you chose to study *Soaring in the Prophetic,* I hope it draws you closer to the Lord Jesus as He stirs your embers to kindle a fire deep within you for a greater anointing in the prophetic gifts.

"For I [Jesus] did not speak of my own accord, but the Father who sent me commanded me what to say and how to say it. I know that his command leads to eternal life. So whatever I say is just what the Father has told me to say." (John 12:49–50)

Acknowledgements

. . . .

A heartfelt and warmest "Thank you!" to the pastors and leaders I have had over the years who most of all taught me to love and esteem both the Word of God and the Spirit of God—A heritage of highest value.

To my husband George, whose knowledge of and love for the Truth has often been a guiding light on my journey, and in writing *Soaring in the Prophetic*. George, thank you for allowing me to soar.

To Holly Dunning, my prayer partner since 2007. I know full well that without your prayer support I would not have finished *Soaring in the Prophetic*. Thank you, Holly, for your friendship, prayers, and our weekly journeys. God has changed lives because we prayed.

And, a huge "Thank you" to Karen Huddleston. Your sensitivity to the Holy Spirit and your labor of love has bailed me out at two very critical times. Thank you for meticulously reading over this manuscript, and for your part in the first *Soaring in the Prophetic* small group. Karen, you are a treasure.

Special "Thanks" to my parents, whose love has always been a green pasture.

Introduction

◆ •

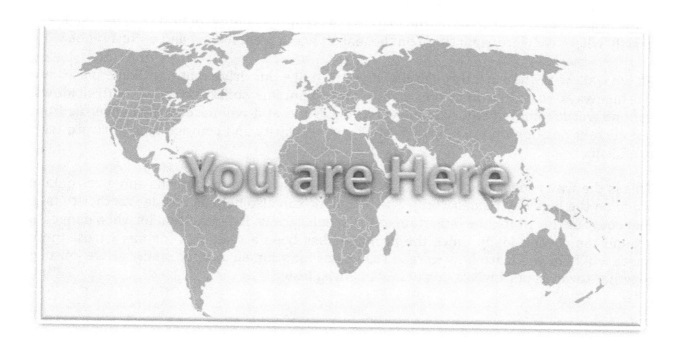

Y ES, YOU ARE "HERE," BUT WHERE IS "HERE"? What about "there"? Moreover, how do we get from "here" to "there"? We need a road map right. A roadmap allows us to avoid roads, which are not direct routes, some of which may even be dangerous, or dead ends. Therefore, we plan our course and start driving. Along the drive, we see signs, which are not on the map such as Speed Limit 65, Sharp Curves Ahead, To Interstate 5 Next Left, and so forth. Road signs are helpful and often critical. They give precision and detail where the map does not and they can warn us of approaching conditions.

Early in the summer of 2012, my husband and I went for a drive. We started out on a main highway and from there we followed a map directing us onto smaller and more remote roads. These roads, though on the map, were not clearly identified and neither were the details of each road's condition. We turned here and there, following the map the whole way. We finally ended up on a dirt road behind a ski resort, used as a ski run during the ski season. The dirt "road" we were on was barely one lane and muddy, with fallen trees across it, and it was very high in the mountains. At one point, I could not get myself to look at the view from our altitude because well, it was scary.

A very long time had passed since we had seen a road sign of any kind and now evening was approaching. I admit I was concerned. Was the road we were on actually the one we thought we were on according to the map? Do we turn around to find the last place we knew for sure? Do we keep going forward? I asked God for a sign (a road sign) and within 30 seconds there it was—a sign—a small sign, but nevertheless a significant sign! Now we knew exactly where we were on the map. We were in the middle of nowhere but we knew exactly where we were, right there on the map. It was a great feeling and quite a relief.

As we walk with the Lord through life, it is much like our drive that day. Some places are like highways, some like dusty dirt roads in the mountains, some like valleys with shadows, yet one word from God will change everything. Not that it will necessarily deliver us from our current position on the map but it will give us clarity and courage to go forward with confidence.

This is the way I see the prophetic. It is not the roadmap but it confirms and gives details while on the highway (Isaiah 35:8). The prophetic can also help us decide whether to take that route or this route, the interstate or the scenic byway. It can caution us when danger is around the corner. Many times the prophetic has been a road sign for me; I trust these pages will help you learn how to read road signs for yourself and for others as we journey together towards our high calling of God in Christ Jesus.

Soaring
in the
Prophetic

Bible Study

Chapter 1

• •

Preparation of the Person

"Call to me and I will answer you and tell you great and
unsearchable things you do not know."
Jeremiah 33:3

And we, who with unveiled faces all reflect the Lord's glory, are
being transformed into his likeness with ever-increasing glory,
which comes from the Lord, who is the Spirit.

2 Corinthians 3:18

Introduction

• •

Preparation of the Person

IS PERSONAL PREPARATION IMPORTANT? How does God view maturity and immaturity; are the immature disqualified from being used by Him? These are some of the topics discussed in this chapter.

An apple farmer once asked his friend to pick out a perfect apple. Of course, she picked a beautiful, red, fat juicy apple. Polishing it off on her soft cotton shirt, she said, "*This* is a perfect apple." As she bit into the crisp apple, juice splashed everywhere. Savoring every bite, she repeated, "This is a perfect apple!" The apple farmer took her out into the orchard. As they walked through the orchard, a warm breeze blew upon them. The farmer noticed a small green immature (and sour) apple still connected to the tree. Pausing to show his friend he said, "This too is a perfect apple—immature, yes, but *perfectly* immature. In time it too will display all the characteristics of the red apple you ate earlier."

What an amazing picture for us who are trying to please our Father. Is He upset with our immaturity? Not at all, He is instead on the sidelines cheering us on. "You can do it," He cheers, as the Holy Spirit takes the Play Book and reveals to us Jesus' Master Plan and our part in it.

God is grieved, however, when we ought to be further along, but because we haven't been keeping in step with the Holy Spirit, we are still babes and need someone to teach us the elementary truths of God's word all over again. When we are in this situation God will deal with us as a Father with His children and use discipline to correct us, as Hebrews 12:1–13 reveals. He may send a prophet to bring a corrective word, He may allow unpleasant circumstances to come our way ("Before I was afflicted I went astray, but now I obey your word." Psalm 119:67) or He may just choose to enlighten our understanding through the written word. Why does He do this? He disciplines us because God loves us. All of His dealings with us are to draw us closer to Him even if it does not seem that way at the time.

Why is personal preparation important?

••

Individual preparation is essential if we are going to hear God and hear Him accurately.

Read the following scriptures in John then respond to the questions below.

"'Father, glorify your name!' Then a voice came from heaven, 'I have glorified it, and will glorify it again.' The crowd that was there and heard it said it had thundered; others said an angel had spoken to him." (John 12:28-29)

1. What did the Father do?

2. What did the people hear?

3. Why?

What really happened? The truth is that the Father spoke, but depending on where each one was personally with God determined whether they recognized His voice. Some thought His voice was a natural phenomenon (thunder), others acknowledged it as supernatural but not knowing exactly what it was (angelic) but Jesus recognized it as God—His Father's voice.

A pastor, presumably understanding in the prophetic once said to me, "Prophecy, true prophecy will pin you to the back of your chair." Is this a true statement? No! Our own hunger and the condition of our own spiritual ears determine what we hear. In fact, the Holy Spirit Himself in Scripture exhorts us repeatedly to "hear what the Spirit is saying." Not all "heard" Jesus when He walked the earth even though He was God manifested in the flesh.

Hunger

God frequently uses the natural world to reveal truth about the spiritual world and the Kingdom of God. He uses everyday things to help us understand the spiritual realm. Jesus often taught the disciples spiritual truths this way. For example, Jesus said, "Blessed are those who hunger and thirst for righteousness, for they will be filled. (Matthew 5:6) Jesus taught the people about spiritual hunger and thirst by relating it to the need and desire for natural food and drink.

First, let us look at natural hunger.

Natural Hunger

1. What is natural hunger?

2. What is likely to happen if you are full?

3. What happens if you eat too much junk food?

Spiritual Hunger

Read Psalm 34:8, Matthew 5:6, and Revelation 3:14–22

AS THE DEER PANTS FOR STREAMS OF WATER, SO MY SOUL PANTS FOR YOU, O GOD. MY SOUL THIRSTS FOR GOD, FOR THE LIVING GOD. WHEN CAN I GO AND MEET WITH GOD? PSALMS 42:1-2

1. What is spiritual hunger?

2. Why do you think some people are not hungry for God?

Read 1 Corinthians 12:31 and 14:1, 12, and then respond to the following questions.

3. What should our attitude be towards spiritual gifts?

4. Why do you think there are not more Christians manifesting spiritual gifts?

5. Which spiritual gifts do you know you have?
(Chapter 6 gives definitions and descriptions for the gifts of the Spirit)

6. Which ones do you want to have?

We began this section by looking at natural hunger in order to set the stage to understand spiritual hunger. For the Christian, spiritual hunger is all that is necessary for the revelatory prophetic gifts of the Spirit. True hunger will draw us to pursuit of spiritual gifts.

When we live off junk food, we get out of shape, unhealthy and sluggish, and the desire for healthy food usually fades. However, with spiritual hunger the more of God we experience the healthier we are. In addition, the more of God we experience the more we want and the more determined we are to get hold of Him. However, worldliness and other passions in our lives will dull the pursuit of God aroused by spiritual hunger (The seed that fell among thorns: Matthew 13:22). We cannot passionately pursue God and the world at the same time.

Paul, when writing to the Corinthians uses words like, be eager, be zealous, and pursue when describing what our attitude should be concerning spiritual gifts. All of us have spiritual gifts; some known and some are dormant. As we discover our gifts and exercise them, maturity and accuracy increase, and so does hunger. In later sections, we study this in more detail.

As we use our gifts, the Lord will give us more. In Luke 19:11–26 the servant did not use what the master had given him so the master judged him for it. The master took away the money from the servant who had not invested his money and gave it to the one who had doubled his. God is looking for us to use what we have in order to receive more. Putting what we already have into use takes courage and faith however, it is necessary for growth. "One man gives freely, yet gains even more; another withholds unduly, but comes to poverty." (Proverbs 11:24) This is a principle of God, not just applying to financial dealings.

> THE ENTIRE CHRISTIAN WALK IS GIVING AWAY WHAT WE HAVE FREELY RECEIVED FROM GOD.

When spiritual gifts are vital and emphasized in the scriptures why then do we not see them operating in church services and in the lives of Christians more often? It could be a lack of understanding or lack of teaching or a lack of hunger, though individually it may be seasonal. Sometimes people just need to be encouraged to stir up again their spiritual gift, rekindling the flame they once had. Paul exhorted Timothy "For this reason I remind you to fan into flame the gift of God, which is in you through the laying on of my hands." (2 Timothy 1:6) If you listen closely, you can hear Paul saying, "Timothy, get hungry again! Pursue spiritual gifts, get passionate, fan the flame, and go after them, Timothy! Fulfill your prophetic call."

Different perspectives exist about when Christians receive gifts of the Spirit. Some believe at birth, some at spiritual birth (salvation), and others when we experience Pentecost and receive the baptism in the Holy Spirit (Acts 2). What we know for sure is the Bible says in 1 Corinthians 12:31 and 14:1 that we are supposed to *earnestly desire* spiritual gifts. That means there are gifts we can have just because we earnestly desire to have them. So, *pursue spiritual gifts.*

Usually the gifts we desire to have are the very gifts God desires us to have (or has given to us already) and our desire to have them is the Lord stirrings within us to pursue those very gifts.

Ask the Holy Spirit to encourage you in His gifts, especially the ones you have passion for and believe God wants you to focus on. For definitions and biblical examples of spiritual gifts, see Chapter 6.

Spiritual Maturity

1 Corinthians 2:6–3:4

1. Who knows and understands the things of God?

2. Who reveals the things of God?

3. How are the things of God discerned?

4. Why were the Corinthians fed only milk?

5. When can God feed us solid food?

6. According to this section, what is worldliness?

Personal Inventory: Reflect on this section. Is there anything God is speaking to you?

"However, as it is written: 'No eye has seen, no ear has heard, no mind has conceived what God has prepared for those who love him' — but God has revealed it to us by his Spirit. The Spirit searches all things, even the deep things of God." (1 Corinthians 2:9–10)

"I [Jesus] have many more things to say to you, but you cannot bear them now. But when He, the Spirit of truth, comes, He will guide you into all the truth; for He will not speak on His own initiative, but whatever He hears, He will speak; and He will disclose to you what is to come. He will glorify Me, for He will take of Mine and will disclose it to you." (John 16:12–14 NAS)

In both of the above scriptures, the Holy Spirit is the one who reveals the things of God to us. Whether milk or meat, the Holy Spirit sets the banquet table of both. Develop a deep relationship with the Holy Spirit. Learn His leading, His voice, His anointing, be His friend, trust Him. He is the Spirit of wisdom and revelation, the one who takes the things of Jesus and reveals them. He searches the depths of God and yet He lives inside of us. We are created for His indwelling, friendship and fellowship—the deep things of God—how worthy they are of the pursuit!

Worldliness will hinder or halt friendship with the Holy Spirit (James 4:4). Worldliness is a bizarre dynamic in a Christian; it is an enigma. It creates a spiritual screening for the deeper wisdom and truths of God. Sadly, the Corinthians disqualified themselves from "solid food" by clinging to the wisdom of the world, and we can too. The two wisdoms are incompatible—milk is what the Corinthians could digest so milk is what God fed them. Babies are so cute, and we do not think twice when a baby messes its diaper or sucks its thumb, but when the baby turns five, ten, or forty and they are still acting the same as they did at two, it is a sign of an illness or a handicap.

> I WAS BORN FOR YOUR ANOINTING, CREATED FOR YOUR DWELLING, A PLACE FOR YOUR SPIRIT, O LORD, I WAS MADE FOR YOU... HOLY SPIRIT, REVEAL THE THINGS OF GOD TO US.

Paul heightens the Corinthians' anticipation for the deeper secret wisdom in chapter 2, the words taught by the Holy Spirit—the meat. Wisdom however is spoken among the mature, expressing spiritual truths in spiritual words. Paul therefore instead digresses to say, "Brothers, I could not address you as spiritual but as worldly—mere infants in Christ. I gave you milk, not solid food, for you were not yet ready for it. Indeed, you are still not ready. You are still worldly. For since, there is jealousy and quarreling among you, are you not worldly? Are you not acting like mere men? For when one says, 'I follow Paul,' and another, 'I follow Apollos,' are you not mere men?" (1 Corinthians 3:1-3)

Jealousy, quarreling—worldliness, are serious sins but since they are abundant in society (and the church) today, they can be easy to ignore in our own heart. Let us not ignore them. They are very dangerous heart attitudes and have the capacity to do great damage, as we will study in the next chapter.

SCENIC BYWAY

Bring 1 Corinthians 2-3 into present day. How do these scriptures fit in your experience? Could it relate to following movements, denominations and people instead for following Christ? Is it easier to follow people or to follow Jesus Christ and the leading of the Holy Spirit? Compare your thoughts to 1 Corinthians 11:1.

1. Why was the author finding it hard to explain the deeper truths to the Hebrews?

2. Who needs milk?

3. Who can eat solid food?

4. What have the mature done?

5. List the elementary teachings of Christ.

Personal Inventory: Which (if any) of these truths do you need to become more acquainted with?

The Hebrews should have been teaching others but instead they needed to go back to Elementary School and learn the foundational teachings all over again. They had a faulty foundation. Foundations determine the type and structure size of the building. If the foundation is undersized, is not plumb, or if it is made of faulty materials, the faulty foundation becomes increasingly obvious and dangerous when the structure is built. This is the reason why God had not authorized the Hebrews a building permit (if God permits 6:3). Cults build on faulty foundations. "For no other foundation can anyone lay than that which is laid, which is Jesus Christ." (1 Corinthians 3:11) Become familiar with the foundational teachings not only to understand them, but also in order to be able to communicate them to others.

I remember a time when we were on our way home from visiting relatives in Nevada. A pickup truck coming towards us was stacked with layers of hay. The first layer was off plumb a little, and with each layer, the hay was tilting more and more. Not only was the hay off plumb but the truck for such a large load was undersized. It was therefore in obvious danger of tipping over, especially if it came to a curve. When I saw the truck of hay the Lord spoke to me along this thought: As long as we are going straight and slow we can be off plumb a little (like the disciples in Luke 10:17-20) but, when trials come (like curves in the road) off plumb can be very destructive. God wants a large building moving forward and advancing, so the foundation and building must be strong and plumb.

Hebrews 5:13 says, "Anyone who lives on milk, being still an infant, is not acquainted (Greek: inexperienced, ignorant, unskillful) with the teaching about righteousness." The teaching about *righteousness:* the teaching about righteousness is *the* foundational doctrine for Christianity. (God the Son—Jesus Christ, lived a sinless life, died for all humanity so that anyone who receives Him would be declared righteous through faith in Him.) Yet, the Hebrews were ignorant of this elementary teaching.

> JESUS CHRIST
> NOTHING MORE
> NOTHING LESS

Anyone who tries to appease the Father by works remains a babe. "I do not set aside the grace of God, for if righteousness could be gained through the law, Christ died for nothing!" (Galatians 2:21) Legalism and self-righteousness unite through works (see Romans 4): justifying ourselves instead of relying upon Jesus. Those who do so will always see the Kingdom and the Father through distorted vision. In order to grow up, the foundation of righteousness must solidify forever in our understanding and experience. No matter how mature people may seem by their words and actions, they are babies—having spiritual cataracts—if they are built on anything but Jesus Christ and His righteousness.

The mature laid a foundation in the elementary principles of Christ, and then by constant use, trained themselves to distinguish good from evil. The only way to gain experience in the prophetic gifts is to exercise our gift(s); by exercising our gifts, we learn the leading of the Holy Spirit. I have made many mistakes, but as I exercised my gifts, I became more accurate. I acted upon what I thought God said and found out if I was right by getting feedback from others and from God. (He has His special little ways of letting us know.)

Hebrews 5:11 says the author wanted to feed them solid food but was unable to because of their spiritual condition—they were dull of hearing. This is the same theme in 1 Corinthians 3:1-3 and John 16:12–14 above. The Holy Spirit will only feed us the deep things of God when we can handle the deep things. Let us be the kind of Christians to whom God issues a building permit.

Philippians 3:8–16

1. According to this passage, what is the one thing worth the loss of all else?

2. What should our attitude be towards our own imperfection?

3. What one thing does Paul do?

4. What "things" does Paul say we are to forget? (How does this apply to us?)

5. In verse 15, Paul says the mature have this "view of things" or "this mind"; what is Paul's point? It may help to list each of the main points in verses 8–16.

Personal Reflection: Is the Holy Spirit is speaking to you about anything from this section? Write down a few notes for personal reflection and prayer.

Paul's personal testimony is on display for all of us to read. He brings to center stage his distinction in the flesh, and then juxtaposes it with how utterly powerless it was to help him before God or to know Him. Paul considers his prestige a deficit because of its ability to tug at him to trust in it rather than in the righteousness of Jesus Christ alone. Looking back on his life, Paul says it was all manure (Greek) compared to the surpassing greatness of knowing Jesus Christ! Paul spent his whole life working on his own righteousness and standing in Judaism. Paul was, according to the Law, blameless: circumcised on the eighth day, of the people of Israel, of the tribe of Benjamin, a Hebrew of Hebrews; concerning the law, a Pharisee; as for zeal, persecuting the church; as for legalistic righteousness, faultless. Paul concludes, "...for we are the circumcision, who worship God in the Spirit, rejoice in Christ Jesus, and have no confidence in the flesh"—no confidence in the flesh! Paul knew, in order to gain Christ he had to consider loss everything else in which he had put his confidence before God.

Can you hear the bellowing from deep within Paul's heart, "Jesus, You are worth the loss of everything! Oh the surpassing greatness of knowing You! I want to know You, Jesus! I want to know the power of Your resurrection! I want to know the fellowship of Your suffering! I want to be conformed to Your death and attain to the resurrection from the dead." Wait, did Paul just say, "...attain to the resurrection of the dead"? Resurrection of the dead, attested to all over the scriptures, is part of our inheritance as believers,—is it not? (Acts 24:15, Romans 6:5, 1 Corinthians 15) What then is Paul saying? Is he implying we can tap into the next age through faith and therefore "attain" to some of what is available in that age? I believe so.

A careful search of the scriptures presents this case. First, I will frame my explanation with Revelation 13:8, "All inhabitants of the earth will worship the beast—all whose names have not been written in the book of life belonging to the Lamb that was slain from the creation of the world." Jesus paid the price, in God's reality, before He created the world. God is timeless; He is not bound by time. He knew man would sin and Jesus paid the price before He created man, though in time the crucifixion was close to 2000 years ago. With this in mind look at these other examples: Moses esteemed the reproach of *Christ* as greater riches than the treasures of Egypt; he endured because he *saw* Him Who is invisible (Hebrews 11); Abraham and David were both justified by faith under the Old Covenant (Romans 4). Also see Titus 1:2, 1 Corinthians 2:7, Ephesians 1:4, 3:9–11, and 1 Peter 1:20; scriptures which all support this view.

Paul concludes this section with a "one thing"; (13–14) "but one thing I do, forgetting those things which are behind and reaching forward to those things which are ahead, I press toward the goal for the prize of the upward call of God in Christ Jesus." He then says, (15) "All of us who are mature should take such a view of things. And if on some point you think differently, that too God will make clear to you." He finishes by saying, (16) "Only let us live up to what we have already attained." Can you hear Paul's passion, "Forget the past; all your failures, all your accomplishments, your pedigree, your education, your self-righteousness; they mean nothing—they are of no value in justifying you before God. If you trust in them they become a ball and chain to infancy." If we want to grow up, we must forget the past and press forward.

This section describes how we should view the past, present and future. The past is to be forgotten, counted as rubbish, and considered all a loss; presently we are to be found in Jesus and with His righteousness, knowing we have not attained our goal but straining (NIV) and reaching (NAS) and pressing toward (the future) knowing Jesus Christ in the deepest way possible and the purpose for which we were created.

How can we mature?

♦ ♦

Read the scriptures and then write why each of these disciplines is necessary to mature.

1. Prayer

Matthew 26:41, Acts 10, 1 Peter 4:7, and Jeremiah 23:21–22, 30:21
1 Corinthians 14:1-14

2. Bible

Psalm 119:9–11, Psalm 138:2, Ephesians 5:25–27, and Matthew 4:1-11

3. Worship

Psalm 95, 1 Samuel 16:23 and 2 Kings 3:15

4. Exercising spiritually

Hebrews 11, Mark 4:1–25

5. Renewal of Mind

2 Corinthians 10:3–6, Colossians 3:1–3, Luke 16:15, Romans 12:1–2

6. Fellowship

Acts 2:42, Hebrews 3:12–13, Hebrews 10:24–25

7. Fasting

Matthew 9:14–15, Daniel 10:1–21, Isaiah 58

1. Prayer   Matthew 26:41, Acts 10, 1 Peter 4:7, and Jeremiah 23:21–22, 30:21, 1 Corinthians 14:1-14

At the heart of prayer is man reaching out to God and God in return, responding to man. For the sake of theological boundaries—man cannot and does not initiate reaching out to God, for it is the Father who draws man to reach out to God (John 6:44, 65); that said, this section will focus on man's reaching and God's responding.

Jeremiah 30:21 is a Messianic prophecy describing the wholehearted devotion of Jesus juxtaposing the lackadaisical heart of humankind. Its intensity is astonishing. The Hebrew includes, "who will mortgage his heart to draw near/approach Me..." Different translations read:
- "I will bring him near and he will come close to me, for who is he who will *devote himself* to be close to me?' declares the LORD." (NIV)
- "...for who is he who would have the *boldness* and would dare <on his own initiative> to approach Me? says the Lord." (AMP)
- "...*risk his life* to approach Me?' declares the LORD." (NAS)
- "...*engaged his heart* to approach unto me? saith the LORD." (KJV)

The Holy Spirit loves to interact with people—Prayer is all about interacting with Him. God transforms us as we pray: His heart becomes more our heart, His thoughts become more our thoughts; we hear Him speak so we pray His will. The more we transform, the more we will pray according to His will and the more we will receive what we ask of Him.

In prayer, God will often reveal His secrets as He did to Peter in Acts 10. (Cornelius also was devoted to prayer and had his vision at the ninth hour: the hour of prayer.) God reveals spiritual realms (which are not for the faint-hearted): people have visited strange places, seen bizarre beings (and had visitations from those beings), and encountered the manifest presence of the Holy Spirit. Prayer is a journey with God. Lives change because someone prayed.

Weekly, since 2007, my close friend Holly and I have prayed together, with very few exceptions. (When we began, there were three of us, but we had to say good-bye to Connie who died of cancer.) We have prayed our five children, our husbands, our churches, extended family members, finances, and the world through the last 6+ years. When we began praying together our oldest boys were in high school and we did not stop even when I moved to Idaho. As we prayed, the Holy Spirit would most often show us His plans—and the enemy's plans too—we then would pray in line with His revelation. The Holy Spirit once told Holly that He altered the lives of our families because we prayed for them. We think, "Of course they have" but think about it—what a profound privilege to have altered the lives of our loved ones because God answered our prayers.

Sometime ago I started a habit of praying for prophetic revelations before meetings and conferences, writing down what the Lord spoke to me and then crossing it off as the Lord revealed whom the words were for. The Holy Spirit once gave me a picture of a very tall African American man—probably 6'10." As the Lord showed him to me I began to pray for him concerning just about anything I could think of from the Book of Nehemiah. At the conference there he was—nearly 6'10" and African American. After a short discourse with him, I explained I had seen him while in prayer and prayed for him about the Book of Nehemiah:

praying for courage, to scale the city's walls at night, not to give into the enemies' tactics, etc. This got his attention. The Lord had told him to move the church (he was the senior pastor) to a risky part of his city, but the other leaders had not "caught the vision." He had spent the last 10 weeks preaching out of Nehemiah trying to impart vision to the church. He was very encouraged to continue with what the Lord has spoken to him.

Jeremiah 23:21–22 says, "I did not send these prophets, yet they have run with their message; I did not speak to them, yet they have prophesied. But if they had stood in my council, they would have proclaimed my words to my people and would have turned them from their evil ways and from their evil deeds." The word "counsel" above is rooted in "intimacy" and "familiar conversation" according to the Hebrew. God is saying if we want to speak His message, we must sit in His circle of familiar friends. Therefore, effectiveness in ministry is linked to hearing God, and hearing God is linked to prayer: intimacy, being a familiar friend.

God does not see as man sees nor does He reward as man or the world rewards, He looks at the heart. 1 Peter 4:7 says to live a self-controlled life and have a self-controlled mind *so that* we can pray. We can fool people for a while as we live prayerlessly, but eventually our dwelling in front of TV instead of the Throne will become evident. Head to the prayer closet often and reap a reward greater than riches and better than any other friendship anyone could imagine. When we honor God with our time, we will not be sorry.

According to 1 Corinthians 14 when people speak/pray in tongues, they edify themselves, speak to God mysteries with the spirit, and pray according to the will of God. God says He wants everyone to speak in tongues. Paul prayed in tongues more than anyone else did.

Finally, there is something to be said for the *discipline* of prayer, if however, it becomes only a discipline then you might as well go shopping.

2. Bible   Psalm 119:9–11, Psalm 138:2, Ephesians 5:25–27, and Matthew 4:1–11

The Name of Jesus heals the sick, raises the dead, expels demons, saves the lost sinner, bends the stiffest knee, comforts the broken, and sets the captives free. The Name above every name—yet He Himself has exalted His word according to His Name—is there anything higher?

Revelation 19:10 says, "For the testimony of Jesus is the spirit of prophecy." The testimony of Jesus is anything to which Jesus would testify. The word "spirit" is "pneuma," translated as the Holy Spirit, a spirit (angelic, human, or demonic), breath, or wind. The word "testimony" has its roots in being a witness in a legal, ethical, or historical sense. So, Revelation 19:10 is saying: prophecy is whatever Jesus Himself would testify to in words carried by the breath or wind of the Holy Spirit.

Genesis 1:2 says the Holy Spirit moved (hovered, brooded) over the waters, the Holy Spirit still moves over water, the water of God's word. When we store up the water of His word in our heart, it becomes a deep well which the Holy Spirit draws from to speak to us. Whatever God speaks will line up with the *principles* found in His word. Everything we believe God is speaking we must screen through these principles. Not everything God speaks is in the Bible, but it will not contradict its principles.

> THE SPIRIT OF PROPHECY IS WHATEVER JESUS HIMSELF WOULD TESTIFY TO IN WORDS CARRIED BY THE BREATH OR WIND OF THE HOLY SPIRIT.

The New Testament often pulls scriptures from the Old Testament out of context (which we would not classify as sound exegesis) but the Holy Spirit can pull scriptures out of context and make them rhema any time He wants to. This is where much of the prophetic comes from. Scriptures taken out of context enter a "do not enter road" unless they are rhema. In addition, much care should be taken when trying to teach a rhema which originated as a scripture *out of context*. It can (not always) be very dangerous. The devil mishandled the scriptures when he confronted Jesus. He quoted scripture out of context without the breath of the Holy Spirit. Many cults do the same.

God often speaks to me by bringing to mind sections of His word. There was a time when I was around a group of believers who seriously bewildered me. They had a significant amount of passion for God, but much of it based on erroneous doctrine. Some of it was heretical. I was frustrated that God did not stop their teaching, since it was injuring people. As I thought about the situation, the Holy Spirit used a section of scripture to speak to me: I saw the number 70 scroll through my mind, and the Lord said, "Yeah, I wanted to change their focus too." I knew exactly what God was saying because of Luke 10. In Luke 10 Jesus sent out the 70. They returned joyfully reporting and emphasizing demons were subject to them. Jesus' replied (paraphrased), "Yes the demons are subject to you but don't focus on that, rather focus on the fact that your names are written in Heaven." The Holy Spirit was saying to me that He uses people who have wrong perspectives and focus. He wants to mature and change them, but He uses them nonetheless. He also told me, "Berta, I will bless things you won't even touch!" I guess He wants to change me too.

Using a Greek Lexicon we will look at three words used in the New Testament that are translated "word": logos, rhema, and graphe:

Logos: used 316 times in the New Testament, defined as "of speech," "in the mind alone" and as "Jesus Christ the Word of God" (see John 1). Logos also denotes "reason, the mental faculty of thinking, a word uttered by a living voice and which embodies a conception or idea." Jesus Christ, the Logos of God is as Hebrews 1:3 declares: "The Son is the radiance of God's glory and the exact representation of his being, sustaining all things by his powerful word (rhema)." Jesus Christ is the Word (Logos) of God; the exact representation of the heart, character and communication of God, and He upholds all things through His spoken rhema.

Rhema: found 70 times in the New Testament and has roots that mean: "to say, to flow." It is defined as "that which is or has been uttered by the living voice [it could be any sound as long as it has definite meaning], the outflow of the mind through the use of speech."

Graphe: used 51 times and translated "Scripture" every time. Graphe is the inked words.

Graphe is the writing. It is the inked on the page. Logos is Jesus Christ. Logos is God revealing Himself through the Word of God, Jesus Christ, whether through His life while on the earth (God manifest in the flesh) or whether through the written Word on the page of the Bible—Logos is the exact communication/expression of God. The Holy Spirit broods over Logos and as He speaks fresh revelation to us through it, Logos becomes rhema. Rhema is not confined to God breathing only upon the written Logos in order to speak to man. Rhema is also any current revelation from God to humanity any way God chooses to speak it—this includes the prophetic gifts. To further help distinguish the difference between logos and rhema here are the three scriptures where they are used in the same sentence (NAS):

- "He who rejects me (Jesus) and does not receive my sayings (rhema) has one who judges him; the word (logos) I spoke is what will judge him at the last day." (John 12:48)
- "While Peter was still speaking these words (rhema), the Holy Spirit fell upon all those who were listening to the message (logos)." (Acts 10:44)
- "...and to the blast of a trumpet and the sound of words (rhema) which sound was such that those who heard begged that no further word (logos) be spoken to them." (Hebrews 12:19)

We can point to our Bible and say accurately, "That is graphe" and "That is logos." However, we cannot say, "That is rhema." As we read the Bible and God breaths freshly upon it, then we can say, "That was rhema to me" because it may or may not be rhema to another. It will always be logos and graphe to everyone. If God speaks to us specifically about where to live or what to buy, that is rhema, not logos, or graphe.

God's word and its absolute authority and importance in our lives cannot be overemphasized. The word of God whether written or spoken is powerful:

Logos Scriptures:
- To cleanse us by the washing of water through the word [logos], both cleansed and continuing to be cleansed, that we will be made into a radiant bride. (Ephesians 5)
- Logos judges the thoughts and intents of our hearts. (Hebrews 4:12)
- Logos is alive and active. (Hebrews 4:12)
- Logos can "build us up and give us an inheritance among all those who are sanctified" (Acts 20:32)
- Jesus' Name is the Word [Logos] of God (Revelation 19:13)
- The word [logos] is truth (John 17:17)
- The word [logos] performs work in us who believe (1 Thessalonians 2:13)
- Logos is eternal and incorruptible, through which we are born again. (1 Peter 1:23)
- Logos preserves heaven and earth (2 Peter 3:7)

Rhema Scriptures:
- The word [rhema] of God is the sword of the Spirit (Ephesians 6). Jesus spoke "it is written" to Satan while He was tempted in the desert. (Matthew 4)
- The rhema of God formed the universe and is upholding and maintaining and guiding and propelling it. (Hebrews 1:3 and Hebrews 11:3)
- Rhema is food (Luke 4:4)
- Faith comes by hearing rhema (Romans 10:17)

Graphe Scriptures:
- "All scripture [graphe] is God-breathed and is useful for teaching, rebuking, correcting, and training in righteousness, so that the man of God may be thoroughly equipped for every good work." (2 Timothy 3:16–17)
- After he [Jesus] was raised from the dead, his disciples recalled what he had said. Then they believed the scripture [graphe] and the words [logos] that Jesus had spoken. (John 2:22)

The word of God whether graphe, logos, or rhema, ignites faith, instills hope, gives strength and courage, speaks life to the despondent, instills vision, and testifies to the things of God.

3. Worship   Psalm 95, 1 Samuel 16:23 and 2 Kings 3:15

> ...And I am constantly reminded of the story of David and yes he was a king, a great leader but in his heart of hearts, he was worshiper of God. And, it was honest heart and transparency before God that he gave the world his greatest gift in the Psalms. David died, his kingdom and Israel fell and passed away but his Psalms remain giving us hope and directing countless millions back to the heart of God. That is what I want.
>
> Ezra Carey

Worship, being defined in Romans 12 as, "offering yourself as a living sacrifice." The NAS translates it this way: "Therefore I urge you, brethren, by the mercies of God, to present your bodies a living and holy sacrifice, acceptable to God, which is your spiritual service of worship." Old Testament people would often offer sacrifices upon alters; Romans 12:1 is a picture of how God wants our whole life to reflect we are a living sacrifices offered to God as worship.

We express our worship to God many different ways and as Romans 12 emphasizes by a life of surrender and devotion to Him. In this section however, I will focus on the expression of worship through music, singing, dance, etc., the bowing of the heart in extravagant surrender before His Majesty our King. These acts of worship—singing, dancing, musical instruments, etc. are fundamental in preparing and tenderizing our heart to hear from the Lord. This is probably why most church services have worship before teaching. David, a man in pursuit of God's heart (Acts 13:22) was at heart, a worshiper first. David penned many of the psalms.

Following is from a teaching, which a man named Gary Bittner taught during the early 1980s. Gary and his wife, Vonnie, are still dear friends of George and mine:

Psalm 95, commonly attributed to King David, shows a progression in worship leading to hearing God's voice. God speaks all the time, but worship—the bowing of the heart—tenderizes the heart of man to hear His voice. Psalm 95 has a flowing progression. Verses 1–5 viewed as an introductory phase of a worship service: singing, shouting, celebratory exuberance, acknowledging His works. Verse 6–7a (in the Hebrew) says three times to bow down or kneel before Him because of who He is and His care for us. Immediately following is hearing His voice and a warning not to harden our heart when He speaks. From the NAS:

- The celebratory phase: Psalm 95:1–5 "O come, let us sing for joy to the Lord, Let us shout joyfully to the rock of our salvation. Let us come before His presence with thanksgiving, Let us shout joyfully to Him with [psalms]. For the Lord is a great God And a great King above all gods, In whose hand are the depths of the earth, The peaks of the mountains are His also. The sea is His, for it was He who made it, and His hands formed the dry land."

- Worship: 6–7a "Come, let us worship and bow down, Let us kneel before the Lord our Maker. For He is our God, And we are the people of His pasture and the sheep of His hand. Today, if you would hear His voice..."

- Hearing His voice: 7b "Today, if you will hear His voice..." Why is, "Today, if you will hear His voice" right in the middle of worship and bowing down? It is because worship leads to hearing God.

- Warning: 8–11 "Do not harden your hearts, as at Meribah, As in the day of Massah in the wilderness, When your fathers tested Me, They tried Me, though they had seen My work. For forty years I loathed that generation, And said they are a people who err in their heart, And they do not know My ways. Therefore I swore in My anger, 'Truly they shall not enter into My rest.'"

This progression has incredible dynamic to create an atmosphere for the presence of God, the manifestation of the gifts of the Spirit, and to hear teaching from the word of God.

2 Kings 3 is another account where music leads to hearing God speak. Three kings—the king of Israel, Judah, and Edom had banded together to attack Moab because Moab had rebelled against Jehoram (the king of Israel) and no longer paid tribute to him. King Jehoram asked for help from Edom and Judah and they came to his aid against Moab. Along the way to attack Moab, the three kings faced dire circumstances: they ran out of water for themselves and their animals. Jehoram believed they were in the grip of the Moabites. Jehoshaphat, king of Judah, however called Elisha for a word from the Lord. Elisha said, "'But now bring me a minstrel.' And it came about, when the minstrel played, that the hand of the Lord came upon him [Elisha]." (2 Kings 3:15 NAS) The hand of the Lord came upon Elisha when the musician played, he then prophesied giving the three kings direction, provision, and strategy by the word of the Lord. Elisha must have been accustomed to hearing God speak when the music played (though this is an assumption), but why else would he have called for the musician when he needed to hear from the Lord?

> HE IS THE KING OF GLORY YET HE RECEIVES PRAISE AND WORSHIP FROM PEOPLE— INADEQUATE AS WE MAY FEEL TO OFFER IT.

Saul was not a prophet or known as one among their company. However, in 1 Samuel 10 we read the Spirit of God would come upon Saul, and he would prophesy when he met up with this group of prophets. Samuel knew these prophets carried musical instruments.

> [Samuel said] "After that you will go to Gibeah of God, where there is a Philistine outpost. As you approach the town, you will meet a procession of prophets coming down from the high place with lyres, tambourines, flutes and harps being played before them, and they will be prophesying. The Spirit of the LORD will come upon you in power, and you will prophesy with them; and you will be changed into a different person." (1 Samuel 10:5–6)

Could it be this is why Saul wanted David in his kingdom? Because Saul remembered back in the beginning, when he first met the prophets how the Spirit of God would come when the music played? Was this why Saul called David to come play his harp when he was in torment, because he remembered the prophets and their music, and how God would come upon him and speak when they played?

> "Whenever the (distressing) spirit from God came upon Saul, David would take his harp and play. Then relief would come to Saul; he would feel better, and the evil spirit would leave him." (1 Samuel 16:23)

This is probably a significant reason why people receive Jesus Christ when they come to church. The enemy cannot handle the worship and leaves the tormented unbeliever for a while—long enough for the person to encounter God and hear the Gospel of Jesus Christ. The Gospel: Jesus Christ is God, was manifest in the flesh, was crucified, was raised in power, and is calling every person to receive Him and so have eternal life. Every church service should offer the Gospel.

A couple months ago, the Lord spoke to me during a worship service about how, when we are singing, all the people are in unity. We agree in our words and speak the same thing as we sing. God then brought this thought into context with Psalm 133. It is no wonder the Holy Spirit and His gifts manifest during worship when Christians are in unity. In view of this, I wonder if alter calls for salvation ("For there the LORD bestows his blessing, even life forevermore") should be given after the worship instead of at the end of church services.

Faith is married to all spiritual growth, both springing from faith and leading to faith. We pursue God in faith; as we pursue Him we grow in faith—from faith to faith. Hebrews 11:39 says the people were all commended because of faith. Faith is not presumption, a nebulous sort of wishful thinking, or a religious bent. Faith has an object: God. Biblical faith is *always* tied to what God has said or is saying, then having actions commensurate. We grow spiritually when we hear God, believe God, and then put into action what He said. The Holy Spirit is always right there helping us to accomplish what He has spoken.

> BIBLICAL FAITH IS ALWAYS TIED TO WHAT GOD HAS SAID OR IS SAYING: LOGOS OR RHEMA.

Risk is an enormous factor with faith. Every time we step out in what we believe God has said or asked of us, there is risk. It may be the risk of embarrassment, money, reputation—you name it. God is not as concerned with our comfort as much as He is in the increase of our faith, spiritual walk and our fruit. As we take risks because we believe the Holy Spirit has spoken to us, God will help us and work everything out for good even when we make mistakes.

Mark 4 has many valuable insights pertaining to spiritual exercise. Jesus said the parable of the sower is the foundation and most basic of all the parables (:13). Seed is scattered in various soil types (heart types) and is the same seed (logos) in all soils, so it is not the seed, which determines the fruit: it is the soil, the heart of the person. The difference between good soil, which bears fruit and the seed among the thorns, is what else grows in the soil (heart) along with the logos. Jesus said the seed among the thorns are those who hear the word; and the cares of this world, the deceitfulness of riches, the desires for other things entering in choke the word (logos), and it becomes unfruitful. In contrast, the seed in the good soil (heart) bears fruit at the rate of 30, 60, or 100. It is our choice if we bear fruit and how much. Maybe it is time to do some weeding.

> THE SOIL NOT THE SEED DETERMINES THE HARVEST.

Jesus also says, "'Consider carefully what you hear,' He continued. 'With the measure you use, it will be measured to you—and even more. Whoever has will be given more; whoever does not have, even what he has will be taken from him.'" (Mark 4:24–25)

God is clear He is looking for an increase. The principle behind these and other scriptures like them is that God gives everyone a measure. Then, as we in faith put to work what He entrusted to us, God adds to it and makes it grow. Remember the parable of the talents? The owner was happy with all the servants except the one who buried his talent in the ground (same Greek word "ghay" used in the parable of the sower denoting the soil or ground of the heart). Even though the servant initially received a talent, since he did nothing with it, the talent was taken away from him and given to the one who had risked the most

Exercising spiritual gifts will cause trials to come our way, which we would otherwise avoid, but stepping out in faith with what we believe to be God is necessary to growth. We learn along the way in God's very own *School of the Spirit.*

5. Renewal of Mind   2 Corinthians 10:3–6, Col 3:1–3, Luke 16:15, and Romans 12:1–2

Controlling our thoughts according to 2 Corinthians 10 is spiritual warfare, and strongholds are mindsets erected in our thinking which are against the knowledge of God. Obedience is taking our thoughts captive—the Greek means we are literally to lead our thoughts away into captivity or to "capture one's mind." We have control over our thinking if the Holy Spirit lives in us. It will be a long hard haul, but we can and must get control of our thought life if we want to be successful at living for and obeying the Lord.

The mind is the central processing unit of the body. Our minds facilitate our emotions, actions, beliefs, and decisions. Battles are won or lost in the mind. The world around us is drifting towards destruction, and we were drifting with it until we received Jesus. Therefore, much of the way we have been "programmed" to think is wrong. 1 John 2:16 says, "For everything in the world—the cravings of sinful man, the lust of his eyes and the boasting of what he has and does—comes not from the Father but from the world." God and the world system are enemies. We must renew our mind in order to know His good perfect and pleasing will. "Do not conform any longer to the pattern of this world, but be transformed by the renewing of your mind. Then you will be able to test and approve what God's will is—his good, pleasing and perfect will." (Romans 12:2)

How do we renew our mind? It is simple but hard. We force our thoughts to believe God's word, the Bible. The Bible says we are to love our enemies. We know in our heart we do not like _____ and we have not been very nice to her either. We say, "God I see this is sin for me to have these feelings for _____. I ask You to forgive me and help me to love _____." Then we start to pray for her. We stop every thought at the door of our mind, which is negative towards her. We do not talk negatively about her. We return blessing for cursing. We may buy her a gift. We set our love on her and eventually our emotions will follow. It starts in the mind with a choice.

If our mind is like toxic soil when God speaks to us, how will we be able to process what He is saying? Think of a glass of water. If we begin with dirty water and pour, enough clean water into the glass—clean in and dirty out—eventually the glass will be thoroughly flushed and full of clean water. This is the thought behind this section—word of God in, wrong thinking out. As we control our thinking, our faith increases; our mind is renewed; we are transformed.

One way God speaks is to place pictures in our mind. (Jeremiah is full of God speaking through pictures.) So, He drops a picture in someone's thinking, but that person's thought life is more like a junkyard than a garden. How will that person be able to determine what God has said, let alone find the picture in the midst of the junkyard? They probably will not even notice there is something in their "inbox" from God. However, if they have trained their mind how to think and are looking for the "You've got mail" message from God, they will more than likely notice the revelation from Him, even if they do not know what to do with it.

> WHY ARE YOU DOWNCAST, O MY SOUL? WHY SO DISTURBED WITHIN ME? PUT YOUR HOPE IN GOD, FOR I WILL YET PRAISE HIM, MY SAVIOR AND MY GOD. PSALM 43:5

In addition, since our emotions follow our thoughts, if we are having a hard time controlling our emotions, we should start in our thought life. As we control our thinking, we will find our emotions will follow. Either we control our thoughts or they will control us.

6. Fellowship   Acts 2:42, Hebrew 3:12–13, Hebrews 10:24–25

The Early Church devoted themselves to four things: the apostles' doctrine, fellowship, the breaking of bread, and prayers. Fellowship is important and spiritual. Malachi 3:16 says, "Then those who feared the LORD talked with each other, and the LORD listened and heard. A scroll of remembrance was written in his presence concerning those who feared the LORD and honored His Name." The Lord listens when we fellowship with each other, and He writes about it in one of His books!

The New Testament has much to say on the "One Another Gospel." The only way to put much of the "one anothers" into practice is to be around one another.

Here are some examples of "one anothers":
- "See to it, brothers, that none of you has a sinful, unbelieving heart that turns away from the living God. But encourage one another daily, as long as it is called Today, so that none of you may be hardened by sin's deceitfulness." (Hebrews 3:12–13)
- "You, my brothers, were called to be free. But do not use your freedom to indulge the sinful nature; rather, serve one another in love." (Galatians 5:13)
- "Bear one another's burdens, and thereby fulfill the law of Christ." (Galatians 6:2 NAS)
- "Submit to one another out of reverence for Christ." (Ephesians 5:21)
- "Therefore encourage one another and build each other up, just as in fact you are doing." (1Thessalonians 5:11)
- "Now that you have purified yourselves by obeying the truth so that you have sincere love for your brothers, love one another deeply, from the heart." (1 Peter 1:22)

Written to believers these scriptures reveal we need each other and can only obey the attitude of the New Testament when we interact with other believers. Think about our society—independence and entertainment dominate. Many people do not share their lives in depth with anyone outside their immediate family, if then. God has called us a body: "Just as each of us has one body with many members, and these members do not all have the same function, so in Christ we who are many form one body, and each member belongs to all the others." (Romans 12:4–5) Jesus said the greatest commandment is to love God and the second is to love your neighbor, and all the law and the prophets hang on these two commandments. "Love one another" is a phrase repeated throughout the New Testament.

Taking Another Look: Hebrews 10:24–25

Let us consider one another. Consider is to perceive, remark, observe, to understand; to consider attentively, fix one's eyes or mind upon.

The context for Hebrews 10:24–25 begins in verse 19 with an overview of the relationship now available to us with God—because of Jesus. Then, without breaking thought, "And let us consider how we may spur one another on toward love and good deeds..." Basically, "Jesus reconciled you to God, now consider others—how to stir them up to love God more and encourage them to overcome." Spend some time considering others. Be led by the Holy Spirit. Who is the Lord putting on your heart in order to stir them up to love and good works?

7. Fasting   Matthew 9:14–15, Daniel 10:1–21, Isaiah 58

Fasting makes you hungry, hungry people get a hold of God, and God gets a hold of them.

Fasting should be a normal part of every Christian's life. It is a discipline and expected (Matthew 9). We all want the benefits of fasting, but the route to the blessings is a tough road to travel. I have heard it said—if shortcuts exist on the road to spiritual maturity, then the shortcuts are paved with fasting. I have to agree. Fasting in my own life has accelerated me into deeper places with God and awakened my spirit in ways which none of the other disciplines have, though each discipline is equally important.

> IF SHORTCUTS EXIST ON THE ROAD TO SPIRITUAL MATURITY; THE SHORTCUTS ARE PAVED WITH FASTING.

Fasting can seem like an odious task, but this outlook is often fueled by viewing fasting unrealistically with only Jesus', Moses' and Elijah's extended complete fasts as our examples. Daniel's fast from "tasty food, meat and wine" (NAS) spurred great spiritual activity as a result. During Daniel's fast he received answered prayer, saw an astonishing vision, had a visitation (some commentaries say it was Jesus Christ who appeared to Daniel, but I doubt Jesus needed help from Michael), and was given one of the most revelatory prophecies about the end times in the Bible. The "man" says, "Do not be afraid, Daniel. Since the first day that you set your mind to gain understanding and to humble yourself before your God, your words were heard, and I have come in response to them. But the prince of the Persian kingdom resisted me twenty-one days. Then Michael, one of the chief princes, came to help me, because I was detained there with the king of Persia." (Daniel 10:12–13) Interesting and profound insights are revealed in these two scriptures about fasting and its ties to the spiritual realm. Remember this was not a 40-day water fast, it was a 21-day abstention from "tasty food, meat and wine" fast.

When I fast from either noon or 3:00 p.m. until the next morning I notice a significant heightened spiritual awareness, and since it is relatively easy, I can fast like this in the midst of other responsibilities. From time to time, the Holy Spirit leads me through seasons of more extended fasts abstaining from certain, activities, entertainment, or foods in contrast to a scheduled discipline. Without the leading of the Holy Spirit, the extended fasts would be nearly impossible for me. Nevertheless, the heightened spiritual alertness and activity spurred by fasting is worth every missed enjoyment!

Isaiah 58 is devoted to fasting and the accompanying blessings of fasting with proper heart and action. Isaiah 58 begins with God juxtaposing His truth against Israel's perception. God brought them to a place where the Israelites would pause and reflect as seen in verse 3: "Why do You [God] not notice…" The steps to blessings for Israel were realization of their present state with repentance of both heart and action; "if you do this then I (God) will do that." Here is a brief outline of Isaiah 58:

- 1–2: Truth revealed
- 3: reflection by Israel
- 4: realization and conviction
- 5: motivation/heart attitude
- 6–7: revelation & obedience
- 8–9a: the promise
- 9b–10a: requirements
- 10b–11: blessing & promise
- 12: vision
- 13: obedience/heart & honoring God
- 14: vision & promise

If fasting has not been a regular part of your life, take some time to ask God where He would like you to start. If there are health concerns, avoid a food fast of any kind without consulting with your doctor first. There are many ways to fast, and food is just one of many.

Conclusion

◆ ◆

Preparation of the Person

Hearing God accurately and then knowing what to do with what we hear is a sign of spiritual maturity. Jesus is the only one who got it right every time! His example to us—hearing first then acting, is a high call indeed. Let us follow His example best as we can, walking where we have attained and pressing forward.

Growing and maturing, as a healthy human being in the natural, is metaphoric to becoming and staying healthy spiritually. As studied, we exercise, eat right, control our activities and mind, etc., to stay fit both spiritually and naturally. The basics in scripture are clear, but they take discipline and usually hard work. The seven disciplines studied are similar to nutritional food groups and each of them necessary and important to being a healthy Christian.

- Prayer
- Bible
- Worship
- Exercising Spiritually
- Renewal of Mind
- Fellowship
- Fasting

A prophecy came over the microphone, "Prepare yourself body, soul, and spirit—before you meet together." God went on to say He could accomplish more during our meetings if we would prepare ourselves in advance of them. This word from God is a treasure chest of wealth. God created people body, soul, and spirit and we need to take care of each. Stan, my first pastor, did a great deal of counseling. While counseling he would ask people if they prayed, read their Bibles, and how much sleep they generally got. What we do to our bodies affects our minds and emotions. Our bodies need sleep, exercise, and nutrition. When we are sleep deprived, constantly eat unhealthy foods (creating sugar highs, caffeine highs, binge—starve cycles), or are inactive, it affects our soul, body, and in turn, our spiritual well-being. In addition, sleep deprivation can masquerade as psychosis. Take care of your whole selves.

"In pointing out these things to the brethren [Timothy], you will be a good servant of Christ Jesus, constantly nourished on the words of the faith and of the sound doctrine which you have been following. But have nothing to do with worldly fables fit only for old women. On the other hand, discipline yourself for the purpose of godliness; for bodily discipline is only of little profit, but godliness is profitable for all things, since it holds promise for the present life and also for the life to come. (1 Timothy 4:6–8 NAS)

Chapter 2

• •

The Heart of the Prophetic

But eagerly desire the greater gifts.
And now I will show you the most excellent way.
1 Corinthians 12:31

Follow the way of love and eagerly desire spiritual gifts,
especially the gift of prophecy.
1 Corinthians 14:1

Introduction

◆◆

The Heart of the Prophetic

HAVE YOU EVER HEARD A PROPHECY that was biblically sound but it just seemed like something was off or missing, much like an out of tune instrument or an out of rhythm troubadour? Often what was missing was love. The lack of love manifests itself through a wrong attitude, wrong motivation, and harshness when God's intent was gentleness, and so on. When God reveals a prophetic word to someone, his or her own personality is involved in speaking it forth. If there is a lack of love, the hearers may have a harder time receiving the message, even though it started as genuine revelation from the Holy Spirit.

Chapter 2, The Heart of the Prophetic, is a study of 1 Corinthians 13, as it appears sandwiched between chapters 12 and 14. Why is 1 Corinthians 13—The Love Chapter— placed between chapters 12 and 14, when both have much to say about spiritual gifts and their operation in the church service? It seems out of place; or does it? 1 Corinthians 13, strategically placed by God right at the heart of chapters 12 and 14, reveals the proper heart with which spiritual gifts are to manifest.

The Corinthians had a lot going for them. They were gifted and zealous, but they were also a problematic church. One of their problems was their attitude toward spiritual gifts and the operation of spiritual gifts during church meetings. Love was not their central motivation. However, because of this, the Apostle Paul in dealing with the Corinthians provides us with the greatest teaching on the subject of spiritual gifts in the New Testament.

Zeal, knowledge, revelation, sacrifices, giving, displays of power, even anointing alone—is not what God is after. He is *always* after the heart. Though these are all good, they are only avenues in which love is to flow and express itself, as are all the gifts of the Spirit. So, let us flow in the gifts of the Spirit, be full of zeal and most of all . . . "But above all these things put on love, which is the bond of perfection." (Colossians 3:14)

"Since you are eager to have spiritual gifts, try to excel in gifts that build up the church."
(1 Corinthians 14:12)

1 Corinthians 13:1–3

• •

The Most Excellent Way

"But eagerly desire the greater gifts. And now I will show you the most excellent way."
(1 Corinthians 12:31)

1 Corinthians 12:31 is the very last scripture in 1 Corinthians 12, and it sets the stage for studying chapter 13 in view of the gifts of the Spirit and (as this study is emphasizing) the prophetic gifts. "Eagerly desire" means "to burn with zeal" in the Greek. The Holy Spirit is instructing us to burn with zeal for the greatest and best gifts, but to do it though love. God intends love to be the culture of the prophetic. If we are to be excellent in prophetic gifts, then the delivery, the attitude in the delivery, and the message itself if given correctly, will not only speak God's word, but also will accurately manifest the heart of God and uphold a culture of love! Cultivate the prophetic in love.

1 Corinthians 13 will be studied scripture by scripture in view of the prophetic. First, we will pan for gold in verses 1–3, and then get out the shovels to excavate the rest of the chapter.

• •

Read the scriptures then answer the following questions.

1. 1 Corinthians 13:1 "If I speak in the tongues of men and of angels, but have not love, I am only a resounding gong or a clanging cymbal."

Write down any insights you have on this scripture.

2. 1 Corinthians 13:2–3 "If I have the gift of prophecy and can fathom all mysteries and all knowledge, and if I have a faith that can move mountains, but have not love, I am nothing. If I give all I possess to the poor and surrender my body to the flames, but have not love, I gain nothing."

Rewrite this scripture personalizing and contemporizing it in your own words.

1 Corinthians 13:1–3 is a declaration of the supremacy of love, and the importance of love as our motivation, attitude, and heart. These three scriptures leave nothing out for either the spiritual or the natural realms. 1 Corinthians 13:1–3 covers prophesying, understanding all mysteries, and having all knowledge and faith; and it expands to the natural realm, giving all to the poor (Luke 18:22), and even the ultimate sacrifice of giving our own life. Then, as if to shout from the heights and bellow from the depths, God declares, "Without love you have nothing and you are nothing." Notice the scripture does not say prophecy is nothing or knowledge is nothing; God says—*without love, we are nothing.*

1 Corinthians 13:1–3 paraphrased:

> If I have the ability to speak for God and can understand all revelation even the most concealed of God's mysteries; if I have done my best to present myself to God unashamed, because I correctly handle the truth; and if I have faith so God moves mountains through me by healings the sick, raising the dead, through miracles, in evangelizing the lost, and in all supernatural displays of His power; but I have not love—I am nothing. And, if I live sacrificially to the point of poverty and in my zeal for God, I become a martyr, but have not love, it profits me nothing, and I die a spiritual beggar.

If you see your heart has been in the wrong place, pause for a while, talk to God and jot down anything He reveals to you so you do not forget what He said. Prayerfully refer back to your notes throughout the study.

SCENIC BYWAY

Topic for discussion: Jonah—A Prophet without Love
Jonah 3:10–4:11 reveals Jonah's heart.
Read these scriptures and then discuss Jonah's life:

Did Jonah prophesy in love?
Did the prophecy accomplish God's intended purpose?
What was Jonah's state of mind at the end of his life?

1 Corinthians 13:4–13

• •

Characteristics of the Prophetic

1 Corinthians 13:4–13 has been divided into 20 distinct characteristics of love. Read the scriptures listed for each characteristic and write how prophetic gifts should operate in view of each one. When applicable, give examples of how this would apply to us as we exercise prophetic gifts. I suggest using a Greek Lexicon to look up the words for their Greek definitions. There is a blank page at the back of this book, providing more room (if needed) for your thoughts.

Example: If the heart of the prophetic is love, and love is patient, then the prophetic is patient. How can we demonstrate patience in the prophetic? I have included examples from the life of Jesus where appropriate, since Jesus Christ is the incarnation of Love Itself. Jesus gave everything to demonstrate God's love. Not only did He pay the ultimate sacrifice of His life, but He also walked out love every day though everything He said and did.

"He [Jesus] is the exact likeness of the unseen God <the visible representation of the invisible>" (Colossians 1:15 Amplified)

"[Jesus] is the sole expression of the glory of God <the Light-being, the out-raying or radiance of the divine>, and He is the perfect imprint and very image of <God's> nature, upholding and maintaining and guiding and propelling the universe by His mighty word of power." (Hebrews 1:3 Amplified)

Love Is Patient

3. Love Is Patient
1 Samuel 10:8, 13:1–14, John 1:14-18, and John 8:3–11

How do these passages help us to understand patience in the prophetic?

What are the differences between Jesus and Saul in the way they each handled their situation.

As soon as Saul finished offering the sacrifice, Samuel arrived. Samuel was not late (he arrived the day he said he would); it was Saul who was impatient. Saul should have trusted God but instead he gave in to circumstances (the people were scattering so he felt compelled to make something happen). We must wait for the right timing and for the anointing to show up. Samuel represented the presence, will, and voice of God, since he was the prophet. Saul also went outside his realm of authority, since Saul, not a priest, did not have the legal right to offer sacrifices. See *Authority* note below for more about realms of authority.

Jesus did not give into pressure as Saul did. He was patient and waited for wisdom from God, "what to say, and how to say it." We don't know for sure what Jesus was doing as He wrote on the ground—maybe He was writing down the sins of those around Him or maybe just waiting for the Holy Spirit to speak to Him? What we know is that Jesus waited and was patient. Then, when Jesus stood up and gave the word of wisdom, it silenced every finger pointing at the adulteress. The stones they held waiting to hurl at her dropped to the ground. Her accusers were gone. The evidence of her guilt was obvious, but Jesus was kind to her and non-condemning. However, He did not dodge her guilt. He told her the truth and what to do, "go and sin no more."

John 1:14 says Jesus was full of both grace and truth. Jesus was in a situation where the truth of the Law spoke of one thing (stoning her), but grace and truth (the antithesis of the Law) was the will and character of God. In this situation of apparent contradiction between Law and grace, how would Jesus handle the adulteress? Only through the wisdom and leading of the Holy Spirit was the perfect heart of God displayed. Times will come when we will face situations where the heart of God rests only in divine unction for the moment (the perfect word of wisdom). We must learn to quiet ourselves in the midst of tension and great assault on our soul in order to produce something—anything—to please the crowd. Do not give in to the pressure whether from a person, the shouts of a crowd, the enemy, or even from your own soul to produce something. Wait for God. He is not stressed. He is not out of control.

God spoke to me once about a friend of mine. We had moved away so I did not see this man very often and just shelved what I had heard from the Lord. Months later, we saw each other at a conference. I told him what the Lord had spoken to me months earlier. It was perfect timing and completely blew him (and me) away that God had spoken the revelation months earlier. God knows everything. He already knew what was in my friend's path and prepared in advance a word of encouragement to help him through difficult times.

◆ ◆

Authority

Paul said to the Corinthian church in 1 Corinthians 9:2, "Even though I may not be an apostle to others, surely I am to you! For you are the seal of my apostleship in the Lord." Paul was an apostle to the Corinthians but that did not give him authority everywhere. We all have realms of authority within our gifting. Think about it this way: A father down the street has authority over his own household but not over yours; they are his family and God gives the father authority in *his* family. This same principle translates into the Kingdom of God. All gifts of the Spirit (even the prophetic gifts) come with realms of authority. We get into trouble if we transgress our realm. Are we a local church prophet, a national prophet, or someone with a prophetic gift but not a prophet? (Provided in chapter 6, is the definition of Prophet.) Stay within your God-given realm of authority in the prophetic, and function in your gift where God has placed you.

We can see this principle in Luke 7:7–9, "'Therefore I [the centurion] did not even think myself worthy to come to you [Jesus]. But say the word, and my servant will be healed. For I also am a man placed under authority, having soldiers under me. And I say to one, 'Go,' and he goes; and to another, 'Come,' and he comes; and to my servant, 'Do this,' and he does it'. When Jesus heard these things, He marveled at him, and turned around and said to the crowd that followed him, 'I say to you, I have not found such great faith, not even in Israel!'" The centurion had great understanding of authority so that even Jesus marveled. However, what if one of the men under the centurion usurped his authority and gave orders as if he was the centurion? It would not go well for that man!

I remember a time our local church started going in a direction neither my husband nor I felt was right. We talked to the leaders and prayed about it for months, but in the end our leaders decided to change denominational membership. For months, we continued to pray asking the Lord as to whether or not the leaders made the right decision. Finally, God spoke to me saying, "I won't tell you because it is outside your realm of authority." That settled it. They had the right to make the decisions they did, they were the authority in the church, and I was not. Our decision now was whether or not we could live with their decisions and continue to flow in the direction the church was going, or whether it was a big enough change of course to part company with the leaders. Authority is a very big deal to God. In our heart we must be able to submit to the authority over us (Heb 13:17) or find other leaders to whom we can. If we stay in a church where we cannot submit to the leaders, we are in disobedience to the Lord in one way or another; either our heart is out of place, or we are in the wrong church, or maybe both.

The Holy Spirit once spoke to me out of 1 Samuel 14 regarding authority and submission. In 1 Samuel 14, Saul was king of Israel and Israel was at war with the Philistines. Saul gave an order to the army not to eat food until evening, which Saul's son, Jonathan, did not hear. All the warriors were famished from fasting during battle. Jonathan, not knowing the order, from his father, King Saul, saw honey and ate some. Jonathan, when told of the king's order knew it was foolish of his father to give such a command during battle. Later in the day, the warriors were so hungry they ate meat with blood, even though it was unlawful for Israel. Saul, when made aware of the army's sin, allowed them to eat lawful meat without the blood. However, Saul then decided to go fight the Philistines again, but without asking the Lord's direction. The priest requested to ask the Lord first. When they inquired, God was silent. Saul recognized God's silence was due to sin. Through the unfolding of events, God revealed He was silent because Jonathan ate honey. Interestingly, Jonathan, the men of Israel, and Saul all sinned but Jonathan's sin was the reason why God was silent. Romans 15:4 says, "For everything that was written in the past was written to teach us, so that through endurance and the encouragement of the Scriptures we might have hope." Let me digress: Saul (the king and therefore the authority) made a decision, which was not from God. Jonathan, even though he did not hear the command, transgressed the authority of the king and God was therefore silent. The point: We will hinder our walk with God if we are in a place where we cannot submit to our leaders' authority—even if they are making bad decisions. We should be open with our leaders, pray for them, check our own heart, (maybe we are in the wrong) but in the end, find another church if we cannot submit to them.

4. Love Is Kind
Jeremiah 9:23–24, Matthew 15:22–28, and Acts 4:8–10

How can we show kindness in the prophetic?

Why do you think Jesus did not initially respond to the Canaanite woman?

The Lord is kind and delights in kindness. Peter, filled with the Holy Spirit, said the healing of the cripple was an act of God's kindness. Now compare the disciples' attitude in Matthew 15:23 with God's kindness. The disciples were annoyed with the Canaanite women and wanted her to leave them alone. I wonder if the reason Jesus remained quiet at first was to draw out the responses of both the disciples and the Canaanite woman. Maybe the disciples misinterpreted Jesus' silence and thought He wanted to get rid of her too; after all, she was a Canaanite—and a woman. However, the Canaanite woman saw it as an opportunity to get what she needed from Jesus in view of the fact that He had not come right out and told her, "No." Then, even after Jesus declared His ministry was only to the lost sheep of the house of Israel, the Canaanite woman still did not give up. It appears she knew the heart of God better than the disciples did. Jesus marveled at her faith and granted her request.

Think again about the adulteress and her accusers from John 8. Jesus could have pointed to each one of the accusers and openly revealed their sin to all. He also could have dealt with the woman publically, but He waited until all the accusers left and spoke to her privately. Jesus dealt kindly with all the people. He allowed their conscience to remain private, preserving their dignity—that is kindness.

I have seen people who operate in high-level prophetic ministries be very kind to people, and I have seen them act more as the disciples did, as if other people were an annoyance. Our lives and ministries must radiate kindness. When speaking, honor people as children of God by preserving their dignity. Sometimes, the initial revelation from the Lord is not the prophetic word we are supposed to speak. It may be the backdrop (the watermark) to give us context for the revelation, for example in Luke 9:46–48, "An argument started among the disciples as to which of them would be the greatest. Jesus, knowing their thoughts (the initial revelation), took a little child and had him stand beside him. Then he said to them (the prophetic—what we are supposed to say), 'Whoever welcomes this little child in my name welcomes me; and whoever welcomes me welcomes the one who sent me. For he who is least among you all— he is the greatest.'" Jesus did not expose everything God had shown Him regarding the argument the disciples had. Jesus did not say, "The Father just showed Me you guys were arguing about who was the greatest." Jesus used the revelation as the backdrop for a prophetic based teaching opportunity instead of exposing their argument and sin.

God spoke to me one night about a very dear friend of mine. She is a very soft spoken, quiet kind of woman, and sweet. The Lord said the communication problem my friend was having with her husband was the way she talked to him and not what she was saying. Within a short time, we had coffee together. She began to explain the troubles in her marriage. She explained what she would say to her husband and how he would respond. What she was saying was accurate and biblical. However, God had told me something—it was *how* she was saying it. Remember, Jesus relied on the Father to tell Him what to say and, how to say it. All it took was, "Friend, it is not what you say but it is how you say it." She saw immediately what God was saying and knew exactly what the Lord meant. Right there she repented and set her heart and mouth to agree with the Lord.

God is kind, and we must be kind if we are going to be like Him, representing Him to others. God is love. Love is kind. Kindness is a fruit of the Holy Spirit. Kindness is a characteristic of the prophetic.

◆ ◆

5. Does Not Envy, Does Not Boast, Is Not Proud
Matthew 6:22–23

Love is supposed to be the motivation for the gifts of the Spirit. But, what if those who are exercising prophetic gifts, instead of being motivated by love, have darkened and ulterior motives? Then, instead of bringing light by depositing true revelation from God, manifesting His heart in speech and attitude, what is said can bring darkness. The "prophetic" no longer becomes an avenue for building up the people of God; instead, it tears down and destroys. This section is not about people who make mistakes (no one is perfect); rather it is about motivation and heart, and who or what accompanies us.

Look up each word in a dictionary and write the definitions.

- Envy:

- Boast:

- Proud:

Read James 3:13–18.
How can these characteristics hinder the prophetic?

Write the words from James 3:13–18, which accompany God's wisdom from above and the words that accompany envy, pride, and boasting in the appropriate circle.

- Envy:
  - to be heated or to boil with desire for what someone else has
- Boast:
  - to boast one's self
  - a self display
  - employing rhetorical embellishments in extolling one's self excessively
- Proud:
  - to make natural, to cause a thing to pass into nature;
  - to inflate, blow up, to cause to swell up
  - to puff up, make proud
  - to be puffed up, to bear one's self loftily, be proud

> HER [WISDOM'S] WAYS ARE PLEASANT WAYS, AND ALL HER PATHS ARE PEACE.
>
> PROVERBS 3:17

According to James 3:15 if we have bitter envy and self-seeking in our hearts, then we live in the realm of a wisdom that is earthly, sensual and/or demonic (the Greek [daimoniodes] includes resembling or proceeding from an evil spirit, demon-like), for where envy and self-seeking exist confusion is present and *every evil thing*.

Is it possible then, for someone who is envious or self-seeking to give a pure word from the Lord (even if the words are biblical) when confusion accompanies these heart attitudes? If a prophetic word is supposed to be from the Lord, but the dominating characteristic surrounding it is confusion, then leaders beware—there may be more you are dealing with than a "prophecy." Ephesians 4:27 says "...and do not give the devil an opportunity." Also Luke 4:13 states, "When the devil had finished all this tempting, he left him [Jesus] until an opportune time." We are the church of God, His body, but we can give a devil an opportunity to wreak havoc in our assembly if we allow this "dark wisdom" to dwell in our heart and therefore in our midst. Sin has an agent—demon or human; sin does not just float in the air. The enemy is attracted to sin. When he smells it, he will hang around in order to stir things up if he can. Therefore, people who are envious and self-seeking are pulling up a chair for a devil (not only in their own lives, but also in their assembly) since they are providing him an opportunity. Do not give the devil an opportunity!

(I do not believe the Bible supports that a demon can live inside a Christian. See Appendix A for more on this subject.)

Contrast the earthy, sensual, demonic wisdom against the wisdom from above, which is pure, peaceable, gentle, willing to yield, full of mercy and good fruits, without partiality or hypocrisy and sown in peace. Having character commensurate to our gifts—even better—surpassing our gifts, is so vitally important.

SCENIC BYWAY

Topic for discussion: Read Matthew 16:13–23

What led Peter to say what he did in verse 22?
Why did Jesus respond the way He did in verse 23?

Love Is Not Rude

8. Is Not Rude
Proverbs 12:18, 15:2, 25:11, and 1 Corinthians 14:40

Define rude:

Write a paragraph that begins with "If I am not rude then I will..."

How does this relate to the prophetic?

Rude is an adjective: crude or rough in form or workmanship; barbarous or ignorant; lacking refinement, culture, or elegance, uncouth, boorish, coarse, vulgar; discourteous, unmannerly; rough, violent, harsh; having or showing little skill or development, primitive; not carefully worked out or finished; not precise. Rude is not just abrupt. It has a wide range of definitions and applications for the prophetic both individually and corporately.

Think about a painting: First, the artist decides to paint a picture, then what to paint. The artist purchases a blank canvas and sketches in a picture. As the painting begins, the picture is rough at first, but by adding more and more details, the painting "matures" until a refined piece of workmanship is finished. Then framed, the picture is ready for others to see. Usually, people mature in the prophetic much like a painting. Most do not start out prophesying in detail and with precise words of knowledge. Some do, most do not. As we learn how to be more sensitive to the Holy Spirit, we will also mature in the way we communicate His revelation. We will become skilled in discerning when and how to speak with care and precision as Jesus did. We will speak words from God resembling beautifully and carefully finished pieces of art from the Master painter; whether speaking publicly, in small group settings, or one on one, we all need to become refined, skillful, and carefully worked out pieces of art, lovingly matured by the Holy Spirit's working.

Not only do we mature as an artist's painting does, but also some prophetic words also initially resemble the sketched image on the Artist's canvas. As we wait on the Lord, He often reveals more, filling in the initial revelation with more details. We prophesy in part because we know in part. Sometimes if we would wait on the Lord for the perfect timing, "the part" may become a larger part. If the anointing is not present, we should carefully consider if it is the right time to speak the prophetic word, which God has spoken to us. It may be only a sketch of what He has to say. He may choose to give us further revelation as we wait. Additionally, tag team prompted prophesying, in which God speaks the near same message to different people from different angles with different details, is incredibly faith building and glorious! Wait for the Lord's anointing and timing, the revelation will have more precision, refinement, and detail.

Much of 1 Corinthians 14 discusses the operation of spiritual gifts within church gatherings. 1 Corinthians 14:40 says (Greek definition added), "But everything should be done in a fitting [in a seemly manner] and orderly [arrangement, a fixed succession observing a fixed time] fashion." Verse 26 offers some details on what should be included in church gatherings, while other verses talk more about how and with what attitude the gifts should operate: all things are to edify. Church gatherings are not a free-for-all. Gifts of the Spirit are to flow with the flow of the service and be orderly. Blurting out a "prophetic message" whenever one feels the need is not decent, in order, or biblical. (See Chapter 5 for more on this subject.) In verse 32, we find people have control over themselves as to when they speak, "the spirits of prophets are subject to the control of prophets." God wrote this. He is not annoyed when people wait for the proper time to speak forth revelation. We may be annoyed, but the Lord is not.

As people of God, whether in view of the prophetic or not, learning to live a life of Love is not Rude, will take a lifetime. Keep in mind *Love is not Rude* does not equate to passivity. John the Baptist was direct, and yet, Jesus said of him, "Among those born of women there has not risen anyone greater than John the Baptist." Paul was direct, and he wrote most of the New Testament. Jesus was direct and He is perfect. The goal is to be like Jesus, hearing and then speaking.

Love is not Self-Seeking

◆ ◆

9. Love Is Not Self-Seeking
John 5:30, 12:49–50, 16:13–15, and 1 Corinthians 14

What do these scriptures disclose concerning both Jesus' and the Holy Spirit's focus?

What is the prophetic seeking and not seeking?

The prophetic seeks to speak what we hear from God, for building up the church and revealing Jesus Christ to the world. The prophetic is a doorway for healing, salvations, revelatory insights, etc., which bring glory to Jesus Christ and help to people. The prophetic, (loosely defined and includes all communication by the Holy Spirit) is always hearing first, and then being led by the Holy Spirit to do something with what we hear. The prophetic gifts are to bring glory to the Lord Jesus Christ and are for the good and benefit of others.

Both Jesus and the Holy Spirit relied upon hearing from God before speaking. Jesus is our example of how to live the Kingdom lifestyle. Jesus only did what He saw the Father doing and only spoke what He heard the Father saying. The Holy Spirit too will speak what He hears and will reveal and declare the things of Jesus to us. Hearing first and then speaking is the very nature of the prophetic. Jesus lived this way, the Holy Spirit ministers this way, and Christians are to seek to live and minister—hearing first and then speaking.

Another commonality Jesus and the Holy Spirit have is they seek to bring glory to another: Jesus to the Father and the Holy Spirit to Jesus. Our heart's desire also must be to seek to bring glory to another—the Lord Jesus Christ. Love is not self-seeking and neither is the prophetic. They are both upward seeking and outward revealing.

Self-centeredness and self-seeking rot the soul. The Bible is full of directives both in principle and as commands that focus on building up and edifying others. Not only is it good for others to be edified, but it is also healthy for the edifier. In addition, as our focus is upon others and glorifying Jesus Christ we will be a much happier people, since self-focus makes our minds terrible places to live. Prophetically gifted people can be self-seeking at the same time. Many self-seekers have gone before us; some have been transformed along the way like James and John (Mark 10:37) and others have not, like Judas. Do not be in this for yourself, you will not find what you are looking for.

> DO NOT BE IN THIS FOR YOURSELF, YOU WILL NOT FIND WHAT YOU ARE LOOKING FOR.

Jesus Christ made Himself of no reputation (Philippians 2). Do we seek a reputation in the prophetic, or is our heart in alignment with that of a servant, like Jesus' heart?

"So also you, since you are zealous of spiritual gifts, seek to abound (excel) for the edification of the church." (1 Corinthians 14:1 NAS)

Love is not Easily Angered

• •

10. Love is not Easily Angered
1 Kings 22:8-24, Matthew 26:67–68, Luke 7:16–26, Galatians 4:16, and James 1:19

What could pave the way for an angry and critical attitude in the life of a prophetic person?

Read Matthew 5:43-48

Finish this sentence, "If I have the character of Jesus I will…"

Some people, even some Christians—even some leaders—really do not want to hear what God has to say, and even though we do not want this to be true, it is. Because not all people want to hear what God has to say, many problems often come to prophetic people. One of the most repeated phrases in the New Testament is, "Let him who has ears to hear, let him hear" or slight variations. When we give a word from the Lord, it is imperative—to the best of our ability—to know we have heard from the Lord. Then, no matter what comes our way, we with integrity will be able to stand before the Lord and give an answer to people. Everyone misses the mark sometimes. Be willing to hear what others are saying. Do not become critical and angry; work as a team and love no matter what! A critical person tears down the very thing God is trying to build—His people and His church. The question, can God count on us to have a loving attitude when we are mistreated? If we are humble and loving, it is much easier for others to talk with us when there are misunderstandings. Our attitude should be that we are in this together. However, if we get offended and angry, even if others end up hearing what God had to say, we may have burned bridges and hurt relationships that are not always easy to repair. Let us just live humbly, loving God and loving people.

Ahab, in I Kings 22, displays an obvious and blatant disrespect for the word of the Lord and for the prophet Micaiah, who carried that word. Ahab, king of Israel, was not in right relationship with God and that is why he hated the prophet and what he said. Do not be surprised if some people hate us, they hated Jesus too. If they hate us, make sure it is for the right reasons.

Herodias Herod's wife hated John the Baptist and had him put in prison because John told the truth about her relationship with Herod, that it was unlawful. When the opportunity arose she had John beheaded. While in prison, John the Baptist, to whom God had given great revelation concerning Jesus being the Christ (see John 1:32–34), needed affirmation again. John told his disciples to go ask Jesus if He is the One. Jesus' reply is expected until we read the last phrase, then it is stunning. Jesus tells John's disciples "Go and tell John the things you have seen and heard: that the blind see, the lame walk, the lepers are cleansed, the deaf hear, the dead are raised, the poor have the gospel preached to them." Then, Jesus says the unexpected: "And blessed is he who is not offended because of me."

The word "offended" is the same word as "scandalized (Greek: skandalizo)." Packed into the last phrase of verse 34, Jesus seems to be saying, (If we listen closely, we will hear Jesus saying it too.) "John, yes I am who you thought I was. Remember you saw the Holy Spirit descend on Me just as the Father told you He would. Now you find yourself in prison. I know you did not think it would be like this, John. Do not lose faith or become angry with Me because of your circumstances. I know you thought I would treat you different by getting you out of prison, but do not become scandalized. Believe in Me, John. Trust My love no matter what comes your way. Don't become offended or scandalized because of your expectations of Me."

Of course, it was not exactly like that, but you get the point. We may get scandalized from time to time when we are in dire circumstances, our own personal prison cell if you will. Let us not get angry with God, but instead trust Him no matter what. When people mistreat us for various reasons follow what Jesus said in Matthew 5:44–45, "But I tell you, love your enemies and pray for those who persecute you, that you may be children of your Father in heaven" and Romans 12:18, "If it is possible, as far as it depends on you, live at peace with everyone."

Sometimes it is not possible.

God is so very kind to show us things beforehand; it helps us to prepare for hard times, which are ahead. There was a time when I was having a very hard time with some people who I thought loved me, but now I am quite sure did not. The Lord showed me a vision in which one of them was ripping his glasses off his face saying, "I can see fine without them!" The Lord then proceeded to say that my husband and I were like lenses to this man and he was not going to listen to what we had to say. He thought he could see fine without us. Our relationship with him quickly deteriorated, and his demeanor towards us changed. He turned on us and began attacking us. Within days after the vision about the glasses, at 5:44 a.m. the doorbell rang. We both flew out of bed and ran down the stairs to find no one at the door. As my head hit the pillow the Holy Spirit whispered, "Behold I stand at the door and knock." Thinking I was over spiritualizing things, I went back to sleep. Later that day, as I was praying, I heard the Lord say clearly, "Matthew 5:44" (note the time the doorbell rang was 5:44). Jesus had rung the doorbell! The Lord was making sure I got the message!

Topic for Discussion:

Discuss Numbers 20:7-12 in view of Acts 7:37. Explain why Moses did not enter the Promised Land.

"My dear brothers, take note of this: Everyone should be quick to listen, slow to speak and slow to become angry, for man's anger does not bring about the righteous life that God desires."
James 1:19–20

11. Love Keeps No Record of Wrongs
Luke 23:33–34, Acts 7:54–60, Proverbs 19:11

Why would God insist that prophetic people do not keep a record of wrongs?

SPEED CHECKED BY RADAR

Read Matthew 18:21–35
What was Jesus' point in addressing Peter's question with "I tell you, not seven times, but seventy-seven times"?

Love Keeps No Record of Wrongs as viewed from a few different perspectives regarding the prophetic. Initially, the prophetic revelation is to be spoken without any naturally known history of the "record of wrongs" regarding the person or group. That is, the revelation must be from God and not from the human soul (naturally known knowledge). Secondly, when a prophetic person, wronged by others receives a revelation, they must relay it from a position of forgiveness and love, not from "a record wrongs." Scars yes, festering wounds, no.

Mixture is easy to add by embellishing the message God has revealed with our own preconceived ideas, attitudes, wounds, and knowledge in relation to a group or a person. This is especially easy if we harbor sin in our heart towards the person or people to whom we are supposed to be prophesying. It is wrong but it happens. Holding offenses in our heart increases the likelihood contamination, mixed or incorrect interpretation, will accompany a revelation from the Holy Spirit: right revelation, wrong interpretation. When this occurs, the prophetic person who received the right word from the Lord now delivers it from his or her own tainted soulish understanding, and consequently it is now no longer the message God actually spoke. Harm is likely when this happens. Keeping ourselves free in forgiveness is paramount. Speak the word of the Lord with no strings attached, saying only what God has said, and with a proper a heart.

With this in mind, let us revisit and compare Jonah and Daniel:

Jonah: think back again, to Jonah. God gave Jonah a prophetic message for Nineveh (even though Jonah hated Nineveh). He knew God was merciful and did not want to judge the Ninevites (Jonah 4:2), so Jonah ran from God. He ran away from Nineveh thinking if he did he would not have to prophesy judgment to the wicked city (Jonah 1:2) giving them an opportunity to repent, and avoid being overthrown (Jonah 3:4). Jonah reluctantly obeyed after God dealt with him. He prophesied the warning; Nineveh repented and God spared the city. Jonah was utterly angered and ended up suicidal, all because he knew Nineveh was wicked and he had preconceived ideas about how God should deal with them. Jonah kept a record of wrongs. Even though Jonah finally obeyed God, what he carried in his heart hindered his prophetic ministry and messed up his life.

Daniel: Babylon besieged Jerusalem when Daniel was young, probably 14, or 15. Daniel was among those taken captive from Jerusalem by Nebuchadnezzar and carried off to Babylon. Daniel was from the Tribe of Judah and could have been royalty (Isaiah 39:7). Daniel 1:3–4 says, "Then the king [Nebuchadnezzar] ordered Ashpenaz, chief of his court officials, to bring in some of the Israelites from the royal family and the nobility—young men without any physical defect, handsome, showing aptitude for every kind of learning, well informed, quick to understand, and qualified to serve in the king's palace. He was to teach them the language and literature of the Babylonians." Daniel and his three friends were in this group of young men. Daniel's family may have been (probably was) killed by the Babylonians. He probably saw gruesome carnage, but Daniel did not let the past dictate his future. He served four kings and was over the sorcerers of Babylon. He may be responsible for the information the wise men followed to find Messiah, Jesus. He had prophecies, dreams, and visions, which span until the end of this age. Daniel could have been bitter and hateful (like Jonah) about the loss of Jerusalem, his family, and his captivity, but instead, he served the Lord (and his kings) with purity and integrity.

Keeping no record of wrongs—forgiveness means keeping no record of wrongs.

The Lord told me once that forgiveness in the most supernatural (spiritual) act a person can do while on the earth. After all, forgiveness is the very act of God to give eternal life to those who receive His Son, Jesus Christ. Because it is supernatural/spiritual in nature, forgiveness is in opposition to carnal mind. When wronged, there are emotions, memories, and wounds, which may still be raw or festering. Wading through the raw and festering can get confusing and hinder our process in forgiving. Forgiveness can be a moment, an event, or can take some time as we renew our mind to obey Christ and choose to forgive.

My husband and I served next to a leader for a couple years. We were broken hearted to find out he really did not love us as we thought. Taking the brunt of the attacks, I ended up in the ER with what I thought was a heart attack. (It was actually just a broken heart.) The biggest problem was he rallied others to join him in his attack against me. I spent over three years trying to forgive him and trying to work through whether or not I was as awful as he all said I was. The worst part was that God was incredibly quiet through it all. I ran for shelter to two beloved pastors (thank you Denny and Gary) who encouraged and helped me, but I still could not get beyond the pain and rawness of the assault. I wanted to forgive. Most of all I wanted to know what God thought, but as I said, He was incredibly quiet. (When He did speak though, it was paramount and life changing.) Finally, one night I had a dream from the Lord. The dream silenced every accusation, changed my heart, and spoke about the present—all in one dream. It was all over! Amazing how God can change in one dream what I could not in three and a half years!

The point is, forgiveness is often hard work (and commanded). Keep at it though, and with the Lord's help, we will forgive. God forgives instantaneously because He loves perfectly, but we are not like Him, perfect in love. We must forgive even if it takes a long time. Every time the case comes to our mind, either by our self, or others, we must choose not to be the judge and jury, and God in the matter. Choose to love—choose to forgive.

Finding one prophetic person without scars from another Christian would be difficult. In fact, finding another Christian without either scars or open wounds from another Christian is probably impossible. James 3:2 in the Amplified says, "For we all often stumble and fall and offend in many things. And if anyone does not offend in speech <never says the wrong things>, he is a fully developed character and a perfect man, able to control his whole body and to curb his entire nature." We all offend; we have all been offended. Choose to love—choose to forgive.

Holding on to offenses is bondage and sin. Not only does the unforgiving hold on to the offense but the offense holds on to the unforgiving, like a ball and chain to a captive. It will wear out its prisoner. Remember Matthew 18 (NAS): "Then Peter came and said to Him, 'Lord, how often shall my brother sin against me and I forgive him? Up to seven times?' Jesus said to him, 'I do not say to you, up to seven times, but up to seventy times seven.'" In a following parable from Matthew 18, Jesus reveals an aspect of the Kingdom of God regarding forgiveness. A wealthy master who forgave one of his servants a great deal—more than he could repay—finds the servant refusing to forgive a small dept to another. The unforgiving servant ends up in prison. (Jesus uses interesting imagery pertaining to an unforgiving person.) Then, Jesus says in Matthew 18:35, "This is how my heavenly Father will treat each of you unless you forgive your brother from your heart."

"You can tell when you are dead—it is when blood and water flow out as people spear you" (John 19:34): blood, analogous of sacrifice; water, of the word. Instead of the natural reactions of the carnal nature when others injure us, we demonstrate Christ-likeness if we are dead to self. We release the offender and forgive every time unforgiving thoughts come into our mind, even if it is 490 times in a day. A friend once said, "You can tell when you have forgiven because the fire goes out." Offenses burn in us and wreak havoc on our soul and body. They affect our relationships with both God and people. Forgive and be set free! The unforgiving person is more the prisoner than the offender is, even if the offender initially was to blame. The enemy is good at trying to keep us in bondage through unforgiveness, but keep at it and the fire will go out. God will help us, but we must *choose* to forgive.

"YOU CAN TELL WHEN YOU ARE DEAD— IT IS WHEN BLOOD AND WATER FLOW OUT AS PEOPLE SPEAR YOU."

If you are in the prison of unforgiveness consider this scripture from Matthew 6:12–15,

> "Forgive us our debts, as we also have forgiven our debtors. And lead us not into temptation, but deliver us from the evil one. For if you forgive men when they sin against you, your heavenly Father will also forgive you. But if you do not forgive men their sins, your Father will not forgive your sins."

Interestingly, "And lead us not into temptation, but deliver us from the evil one," is preceded and succeeded by Jesus' instruction on forgiveness. Also, three small but significant words: "as" (*as* we forgive out debtors), "For" (*For* if you forgive... [then implied] your Heavenly Father will also forgive you), and "But" (*But* if you do not... [then implied] your Heavenly Father will not forgive you...). Jesus appears to be saying, we walk into temptation (we open a door to the enemy) when we do not forgive (this would coincide easily with Matthew 18 above). Additionally, we put ourselves into a place of special dealing by God, since He will not just leave us to rot in our unforgiveness, but will hand us over to prison in order to get our attention. Prison is not freedom.

Choose to love—choose to forgive.

Selah:
If this has been a hard section for you, take some time to talk to God. Ask Him to help you forgive and allow Him to cut the ball and chain off you, and get some much-needed rest.

SCENIC BYWAY

Topic for Discussion:

Do you believe Steven's prayer in Acts 7:60 had any effect on Saul's encounter with Jesus and his conversion in Acts 9? View this in the context of John 20: 23.

12. Love Does Not Delight in Evil but Rejoices with the Truth
1 Samuel 15:10–16:1, Galatians 6:1

Why and or when would a prophetic person be tempted to rejoice in evil?

When God reveals sin, what should be the heart of the prophetic person?

Prophetic people can become so enthusiastic about hearing God they disconnect from the people being ministering to and their situation. If this disconnection happens, we can end up speaking the right words with the wrong heart. Instead of being helpful, what we say then ends up being hurtful. Love never rejoices when it encounters sin, evil, injustice, and unrighteousness. A person might, but love never will, even when revealed though a prophetic revelation. We cannot make the revelation the object. The people (or person) are the focus and the revelation is only a tool God has put into our hand for their benefit. Our hearts should break when the Holy Spirit reveals sin in another person's life. Remember Jesus with the woman caught in adultery from John 8 (Chapter 2, *Love is Patient*). Jesus was careful and deliberate, full of grace and truth. He told her the truth, but spoke the truth in love.

The Prophet Samuel's heart was broken when the Lord told him about Saul's disobedience in turning away from the Lord. Samuel was grieved over Saul and spent all night crying out to the Lord. Only then, after a sleepless night, did he go speak to the backslidden king about his disobedience. Samuel was precise in his wording and was able to see beyond Saul's bluff when he said (paraphrased), "It is all for the Lord...even my disobedience!"

Samuel was in a very difficult situation. What was he supposed to do as God's prophet, and at the same time honor a fallen king, established by God? After a series of events, God again steps in, this time to speak to a mourning prophet. "The LORD said to Samuel, 'How long will you mourn for Saul, since I have rejected him as king over Israel? Fill your horn with oil and be on your way; I am sending you to Jesse of Bethlehem. I have chosen one of his sons to be king.'"

Samuel's mourning heart should be the heart of every prophetic person when they encounter disobedience, evil, and sin. Are we such a people, that we would cry out to God all night? Galatians 6:1 says, "Brothers, if someone is caught in a sin, you who are spiritual should restore him gently. But watch yourself, or you also may be tempted." How easy it would have been for Saul's excuses and justification (15:13–15) to side track Samuel. Nevertheless, 15:16 is revealing, "'Stop!' Samuel said to Saul. 'Let me tell you what the LORD said to me last night.'" When? What had Samuel been doing *last night?* Samuel had been crying out to the Lord all night! The Lord told Samuel during the night the details surrounding Saul's sin therefore, when Samuel talked with Saul the next day, he had no doubt of the facts.

Galatians 6 says, "...you who are spiritual should restore him..." Spiritual means essentially: "one who is filled with and governed by the Spirit of God." So, we who are filled with and governed by the Spirit of God, we are the ones to whom God will most likely reveal a revelation of this nature. If God speaks to us a revelation about someone's sin, it would be wise to take another person along if we are supposed to talk to him or her. There may be times when we cannot take another person with us, say if God reveals something like this to us while in the market place. Just be careful, we do not practice with something this important—be careful, be right! If we are wrong, we can injure people. However if we are right then the Kingdom of God will have invaded a life or lives. In situations like this, the Holy Spirit, will most likely lead us in very precise ways in order to communicate the revelation exactly as He wants. Be sensitive to His leading.

Summer of 2012: it was just a shopping trip—abruptly interrupted by the voice of God. Approaching an intersection, the light turned to yellow, and then to red. While waiting for the red light to turn green, a young pedestrian started into the cross walk. He caught my attention as he walked past my car. He was a college-aged man; his head was down, he just looked sad. Unexpectedly, the Holy Spirit revealed this young man's thoughts. The Lord said he was, as a very young boy (about 5 years old), called to the ministry. Now he found himself deep in sin and wondering if he had gone too far into darkness and away from the Lord. He wondered if God's call was only history. He walked into a convenience store as my light turned green. Knowing God orchestrated events at that intersection, at that time, to give this young man His message, I turned my car around to meet up with him in the parking lot. "Hi, my name is Berta. I am a Christian and as you walked in front of my car, God spoke something to me for you. Is it okay if I share it with you?" He was eager to hear what God would have to say to him. I told him exactly what God had revealed and his response was, "You've got the right guy." His parents raised him as a Christian, but he was now far away and deep in sin. After encouraging him to pursue the Lord and inviting him to church, he walked away knowing God loved him, had not forgotten or given up on him, or removed His call from his life.

Another time a man at church caught my attention. In an instant, I saw a motion picture of him standing in front of a mirror, rubbing his face and having a very hard time looking at his reflection. The Lord told me this man was ashamed of himself and he could not stand to look at his reflection in the mirror. However, the Lord wanted to encourage him that He could make everything work out for good. The past was the past and the way he saw himself was not the way God saw him. I found a time to talk to this man and his wife alone. I shared what the Lord has shown me and told him what the Lord had said. He began to cry. He and his daughter were estranged and now he had a granddaughter who was ill. He wanted to go to his daughter and pray for his granddaughter, but he felt he could not because the relationship with his daughter was so very bad. Because of what the Lord said, he called his daughter that day. They agreed upon a visit for the following weekend. The next time I saw him, he and his wife came over to tell me God completely restored the relationship with his daughter, and he had been able to pray for his granddaughter. God uses the prophetic to change lives. God is so very good!

Both of the above stories were situations that were too big of a problem for the individuals to fix or figure out. They needed hope in their dire situations—they needed a word from God. The prophetic is incredibly powerful to help people walk away from sin and to restore relationships. The Lord uses the prophetic to reach His loved ones in their darkest hour or deepest pit, to shed light where there seems to be none. Be available to be His voice.

Love Always Protects

◆ ◆

13. Love Always Protects
2 Chronicle 36:15, Matthew 18:15-17, 1 Peter 4:8, and James 5:19–20

How is the prophetic protective?

If the prophetic revelation God spoke to you, if exposed publically, could embarrass another what should you do?

Love always protects thus, the prophetic always protects. "Protects," also translated "bears," is from a root word meaning to cover as the roof of a house covers the house. It means deck, thatch, to cover—to protect or keep by covering, to preserve; to cover over with silence; to keep secret; to hide, conceal. Therefore, the prophetic covers and protects the person from harm and exposure while maintaining privacy, dignity, and safety. We will look at *The Prophetic Always Protects* from these two perspectives:

> ➢ The Holy Spirit uses the prophetic to reveal sin while protecting the person's or persons' privacy and dignity as much as possible.
> ➢ The Holy Spirit uses the prophetic to protect a person or persons by issuing warnings. Thus, preventing harm by avoiding unnecessary trials, temptations, and dangers.

The Prophetic Always Protects—Love does not expose people unnecessarily

Matthew 18, in principle, reveals the default way to handle sin. He reveals sin publically only as a last resort and only then, usually by someone holding one of the five-fold governmental positions in the church. (For more on the governmental gifts see Chapter 6.) God exposes sin publically in hopes of jarring the persons or a person into repentance (and sometimes as a warning to others). It is, therefore, in their best interest, though painful it may be. God loves people; love covers, and—love does not expose sin unnecessarily.

If the Holy Spirit reveals a prophetic revelation to us that could embarrass someone, do not speak it publicly—what if we are wrong? We have publicly humiliated someone, and even if we apologize and admit we were wrong, thoughts planted in the hearers' minds are impossible to uproot. I have seen this happen. It was over 25 years ago and I still remember the details. My friend's face—the emotion, the shock—branded in my mind forever. The "prophecy" was inaccurate and my friend was completely humiliated. Bets are I am not the only one who still remembers. Gentle, but public correction should have come immediately to this "word," or at least through the course of the meetings.

Wait to hear the rest of what God has to say when He reveals a prophetic revelation, which could expose, embarrass, or humiliate someone. It is imperative that we wait. He will show us a way to minister the revelation in a constructive way that will bring repentance, healing, impart hope, and reveal the love of God. For example, let us say God shows us someone who is fornicating. What do we do? What is God's heart? God's heart is *always* to turn people from sin. His ultimate purpose is to have that person in right relationship to Him—God wants restoration. Wisdom, gentleness, and love are necessary for restoration. Remember Galatians 6:1, "Brothers, if someone is caught in a sin, you who are spiritual should restore him gently. But watch yourself, or you also may be tempted." Knowing there is sin is not the answer, everyone has sin. Bringing God's heart, by way of the prophetic, into the life of the person or persons—leading to repentance, resulting in restoration—that is the ministry of the prophetic!

God has revealed sin throughout the Bible. Following are biblical examples of where God exposed sin publically, privately, or individually, and sometimes, not at all.
- Nathan prophesied to King David privately exposing his sin. God had given David months to repent, but he kept heaping sin higher and higher. (2 Samuel 12)
- Jesus spoke privately to the Samaritan woman about her many husbands and her current sin. (John 4)

- Jesus preserved the dignity of the woman caught in adultery. (John 8)
- Jesus, knowing Judas' many sins, did not expose him publicly. Judas was a thief, he stole from the other apostles, his betrayal plans, and his ties with the Pharisees and Satan; all Judas' sins Jesus kept private. Jesus even continued to let Judas carry the moneybag.
- Jesus continually exposed the sin of Pharisees and Sadducees publically.
- God judged Ananias and Sepphria, on the spot, publically. (Acts 5)
- In the Corinthian church, a man was exposed and excommunicated for having sex with his father's wife. Later when he repented, he was restored and comforted. This is a great example of God's plan for exposing sin. (1 Corinthians 5:1–5 and 2 Corinthians 2:5–8)

Love Always Protects—the issuing of warning for the preservation from harms and dangers

> The Holy Spirit uses the prophetic to protect a person or persons by issuing warnings, preventing harm by avoiding unnecessary trials, temptations, and dangers

It is easy for anyone who has spent much time in the Bible to think of times where the prophetic protected people from danger. Throughout the Old Testament we read about the prophets who warned Jerusalem repeatedly of impending danger if she did not repent. We read of Moses, who prophesied to Pharaoh about the judgments God would send if Pharaoh would not let God's people serve Him in the wilderness. Even to the very last book, *The Revelation of Jesus Christ* prophesies many warnings—including warnings to the churches (chapters 2 and 3) of the consequences if they would not repent of their sins exposed by Jesus.

Following are biblical examples where God used the prophetic to announce warnings:
- Pharaoh's prophetic dream about seven fat cows and the seven skinny cows, which Joseph interpreted, saved nations. (Genesis 41:1–44)
- God issued Nebuchadnezzar a personal warning, described this way, "These were the visions of my head while on my bed: I was looking, and behold..." (Daniel 4:9–33).
- Moses prophesied to Pharaoh national warnings. (Exodus 7–12)
- Jonah prophesied to Nineveh a national warning that led to Nineveh's preservation.
- Many Old Testament prophets prophesied to Israel national warnings to repent.
- Matthew 24 is a national and global warning. Jesus warns Jerusalem of impending danger, partially fulfilled in AD 70. The entire fulfillment is still on the horizon of time.
- In Matthew 2:12, wise men from the east were warned though a dream not to return to Herod, therefore they returned home by another route.
- Paul's [A]angel appeared to him giving warning and instruction in Acts 27:9–44. Thus, Paul was able to protect the lives of all who would otherwise have perished.
- Agabas, the prophet, prophesied to Paul in Acts 21 that danger awaited him if he went to Jerusalem.
- The *Revelation of Jesus Christ* is full of both personal and global warnings.

Topic for discussion: Acts 21:4, 21:11–14

Should Paul have gone to Jerusalem?

Love Always Trusts

◆ ◆

14. Love Always Trusts
Matthew 16:13–23, Luke 24:13–35 (emphasis on verse 27), and 1 Corinthians 14:24–25

How do you think the prophetic leads us to trust God more?

EMMAUS ROAD

When should we believe prophetic words from others?

Since love always trusts, the prophetic is a tool God uses to lead people to a place of trusting Him more. Spurring people to trust God is central to the prophetic. Some will trust God for the very first time because the prophetic revealed the secrets of their heart as described in 1 Corinthians 14. Prophetic revelations speak to past, present, and future circumstances and events—all intended to lead people to trust God more. When God reveals the future, it is not only so people can prepare, but also so that people will have assurance and trust Him during the unfolding of events, confident He already knew the future and is sovereign over all.

Think about the scriptures Jesus must have been revealing as they walked together on the Emmaus Road, maybe Isaiah 9:6–8, 42, and 53. Verse 27 says Jesus explained to them the scriptures that testified about Himself. (Surely, they had to be prophetic passages.) His intent must have been to reveal Himself through the scriptures in order to instill trust in them that Jesus was indeed the Messiah—the Christ and not just a prophet as they thought.

During a group prophetic session, a woman sat in our chair. As we began to pray for her, I saw a prophetic video in my spirit. It was of an 11-year old, blonde-haired girl crying out to God for someone to help her learn how to be a young woman. By revelation, I knew this little girl had no one to help her learn etiquette, how to conduct herself with boys, how to have hygiene, or any of the other virtuous things little girls need help with from their mommy. I began to prophesy to the woman who sat in our chair about a ministry helping young girls, teaching them about how to be godly young women, and of the prophetic video God had showed me. She burst out in great passion, "That is me! That was me when I was an 11-year old girl. I cried to God because I had no one to help me." Unbeknownst to any of us, this woman had started a ministry of helping young girls exactly as had been prophesied to her. The picture the Lord showed was incredibly healing to her. She was overwhelmed that after all these years God was affirming He saw her when she cried out to Him as an 11-year old girl. She knew her ministry to these young girls was not just a good idea, but directed by the Lord instead. It prompted great encouragement and confidence to continue forward.

Are we supposed to trust others prophetic words? If so, how do we know when to trust them and when not to? We are supposed to love God and love people, but are we always supposed to trust what people say? When it comes to receiving prophetic words, ultimately we should trust the abiding anointing as stated in 1 John 2 and screen everything though Him. Even the best and most well—intentioned prophetic people sometimes err, and sometimes, unbelievers get a word from God. (Pharaoh Genesis 41, King Belshazzar, Nebuchadnezzar Daniel 4, Daniel 5) So, "Do not quench the Spirit. Do not despise prophecies. Test everything. Hold on to the good." (1 Thessalonians 5:19-21)

> DO NOT QUENCH THE SPIRIT. DO NOT DESPISE PROPHECIES. TEST EVERYTHING. HOLD ON TO THE GOOD.
> 1 THESSALONIANS 5:21

Think back again to Peter and his revelation from the Father concerning Jesus being the Christ. Following this greatest of all revelations, Peter made a huge mistake of trying to give Jesus "good" advice. Jesus then rebuked the spirit that prompted Peter to make that statement. My point? In Matthew 16, Peter goes straight from the Father's revelation to carnal wisdom—spurred by the devil in just a couple scriptures. So, how can we discern what is from God, what is from the enemy, and what is just natural man? What do we trust?

When talking about the prophetic this is a very important question. First, is it biblical? This is the first question to ask, but it is not enough. Is it biblical, is it anointed, and is my spirit, through the abiding anointing (1 John 2 as stated above), in agreement with it? These are the right questions. However, if the word does not "sit well" it does not necessarily mean it is not from God. Quickly tossing to the garbage bin something that does not initially make sense to us may mean missing a word from the Holy Spirit. Sit on the word for a while. God may reveal something that was overlooked at first glance. Asking questions of the person who gave us the revelation is often helpful, too. The revelation may have been correct, but the interpretation was not. Another possibility is that for some reason we are not hearing well. Brokenness, depression, and other emotions can easily hinder our ability to hear and recognize the Holy Spirit when He speaks. Consider that Jesus always spoke truth to the disciples, and they often did not understand what He had said until Jesus explained it, if then.

God has given us the Holy Spirit so that we might know the things of God. He is our guide into all truth. He can be trusted.

- "However, as it is written: 'No eye has seen, no ear has heard, no mind has conceived what God has prepared for those who love him' — but God has revealed it to us by his Spirit. The Spirit searches all things, even the deep things of God. For who among men knows the thoughts of a man except the man's spirit within him? In the same way no one knows the thoughts of God except the Spirit of God. We have not received the spirit of the world but the Spirit who is from God, that we may understand what God has freely given us. This is what we speak, not in words taught us by human wisdom but in words taught by the Spirit, expressing spiritual truths in spiritual words.'" (1 Corinthians 2:9–13)

- "As for you, the anointing you received from him remains in you, and you do not need anyone to teach you. But as his anointing teaches you about all things and as that anointing is real, not counterfeit— just as it has taught you, remain in him. (1 John 2:27)

Back in the 90's, we were in a small group of about 20 people, two of which were a couple with three young children. The husband had quit his job and they were living with his wife's family while he went back to school for his PhD. During worship, he put his hands over his face and bowed his face to the ground. As he did, I heard his thoughts by the Holy Spirit's revelation, "Oh God, what have I done?" The Lord told me, He has led this man to go back to school but now, in the heat of the drudgery, he was severely questioning what he had done and what he believed God had told him. I told him privately what the Lord had revealed to me as he bowed his head, and the encouragement the Lord had for him. Those were his exact thoughts. He was greatly encouraged, not entertaining again whether or not God had led his family. Although it was a difficult route, they were in it with the Lord.

In my 32+ years experience in the prophetic, I have seen many reasons why some people have given up on the prophetic. Lack of trust in the prophetic gifts is often the result of overzealous, miss-guided, or power hungry Christians who simply heard incorrectly and ended up hurting the gift's reputation. Sometimes there was an impression but someone prophesied as if it was God's audible voice from Heaven. Maybe there was a thought, which was not God at all, but was prophesied as though it was a high-level revelation. Integrity in the prophetic is paramount. If we hear an impression, relay it as an impression, if an audible voice, then as an audible voice. Acts 15:28 says, "It seemed good to the Holy Spirit and to us..." True Holy Spirit revelation can be that it just *seems good*. How a message was heard does or does not legitimize whether or not it is from God. It depends upon whether or not God actually spoke.

◆ ◆

15. Always Hopes
Read Daniel 9:1–3

Why do you think this prophecy would give the people of Daniel's time hope?

Luke 22:31–34, 22:55–62

How can God use prophetic gifts deposit hope in us?

God's perspective, a perspective we otherwise would not have, is the fruit of the prophetic. God speaks about the past, present, and future as Isaiah 46:9–10 says, "Remember the former things, those of long ago; I am God, and there is no other; I am God, and there is none like Me. I make known the end from the beginning, from ancient times, what is still to come. I say: My purpose will stand, and I will do all that I please." God often speaks to us before a very hard season so we can prepare through prayer and anchor the hard season to hope.

Daniel was reading the *Prophet Jeremiah* and understood from the scriptures the desolation of Jerusalem was going to last 70 years. Jeremiah's prophecy spoken 66 years earlier in 605 BC, revealed only four years (nearing the end of Jerusalem's desolation) until the prophecy's fulfillment, since it was now 539 BC. Daniel set his face toward the Lord to make request by prayer and supplications with fasting, sackcloth, and ashes. Daniel believed the word of the Lord, so he acted upon it through prayer and supplications with fasting, sackcloth, and ashes: faith and works working together. What hope this must have brought to the Jews to know their time was four years away!

Reflect on the account of Peter and try to look at it from his perspective. Jesus tells Peter that Satan had asked to sift him (Greek: figuratively by inward agitation to try one's faith to the verge of overthrow), but Jesus told Peter He had prayed for him so his faith would not fail. Jesus then says, "And when you have turned back, strengthen your brothers." In the end, the sifting Peter would go through equipped him to strengthen his brothers, and thus, thrust him into a leadership role. Nevertheless, to get to that point Peter denies Jesus three times, and the third time immediately (while he was still speaking) the rooster crowed. Then—this piercing phrase from Luke 22:61, "The Lord turned and looked straight at Peter. Then Peter remembered the word the Lord had spoken to him: 'Before the rooster crows today, you will disown me three times.'" Peter, broken and probably ashamed, went out and wept bitterly.

Heart wrenching even to read, what must Peter have felt? Jesus knew Peter would deny Him and prophesied it to Peter beforehand. Jesus also saw through the sifting, the denying, and the weeping; Jesus saw the work the Holy Spirit would accomplish in Peter when he returned to Him. God would work it all out for good. Peter remembered what Jesus had prophesied to him about the rooster. However, the whole account of what Jesus said to Peter is in the Bible; so, Peter must have also remembered the part about returning and strengthening his brothers, too. What incredible hope Jesus' prophecy must have brought to Peter in his darkest hour of denying the Lord, and then Jesus looking at him just as he denied Him the third time—how penetrating His eyes must have been! Such pain coupled with such hope—that is God!

A friend of mine was getting close to her due date and was having a miserable pregnancy. The Holy Spirit told me her baby was going to be born on a certain date, the date came, and she had to have a C-section due to complications. One of her relatives was giving her a very hard time about the C-section and was instilling tremendous fear into an already stressful day. I reminded her God had already said her baby would be born that day. Fear vanished, peace flooded, and her son was born that very day.

As I began to pray for a woman, I saw a 17-year old girl who looked exactly like the woman I was praying for, only younger. When I told her, she exclaimed, "It's my daughter! She's backslidden!" What hope it brought to this woman to know God cared enough to show her daughter to me prophetically! We prayed for her daughter together as streams of tears flowed down her cheeks. She left knowing God loved her daughter, and was involved in her life.

Love Always Perseveres

16. Always Perseveres
Isaiah 55:8–11, John 21:15–19, Revelation 2:8–11

How do the prophetic gifts help us persevere?

Why does God reveal the future if it is scary?

God's words both persevere and they encourage persevering. Often without the prophetic word, people would become weary in trials and wander though life. However, when the word of God comes it brings courage, precision, and focus in order that we might persevere through what lies ahead. Even when we have failed miserably, God's prophetic word helps us keep going.

God's words are unstoppable arrows splicing through eons of time until they find a resting place in their fulfillment. God spoke in the beginning of Genesis concerning both the coming of Messiah and the end of this age. Isaiah 55:11 (NAS) says, "So will My word be which goes forth from My mouth; It will not return to Me empty, Without accomplishing what I desire, And without succeeding in the matter for which I sent it." God's words, whether in the Bible or spoken to us prophetically, will accomplish what God said they would. His words, not our words, not man's words—God's words are living and active—only His words.

> HIS WORDS ARE UNSTOPPABLE ARROWS SLICING THOUGH EONS OF TIME UNTIL THEY FIND A RESTING PLACE IN THEIR FULFILLMENT.

God does not reveal the future to entertain or to scare us, but for a purpose. Jesus told Peter in John 21 to feed His sheep, and then prophesied to Peter he would die a martyr and in so doing would glorify God. I bet Peter remembered this prophecy when he was in the very hour of martyrdom and gained strength to persevere because of it. Peter also had time between the prophecy and its fulfillment to gain courage to persevere by purposing in his heart not to fail Jesus as he did the first time. Interesting how God transforms our failures into building blocks of character and determination. It is so like the Lord, He loves to transform.

Jesus prophesied to the Smyrna Church in the *Book of Revelation* that trials and persecutions were ahead, but if they would persevere, a crown of life awaited them. Interestingly, Jesus identifies Himself as *the One Who was dead but now is alive*. This identity corresponds directly with His prophecy to them: "Do not be afraid of what you are about to suffer. I tell you, the devil will put some of you in prison to test you, and you will suffer persecution for ten days. Be faithful, even to the point of death, and I will give you the crown of life." Reflect on all the good Jesus' prophecy would produce by revealing the future to the Smyrna Church beforehand. The overwhelming theme is "I AM sovereign. I know who you are, where you are, your trials and what awaits you; but preserve to the end, it is worth the reward!"

Jesus reveals to the Smyrna church:
- He identifies with them as the One Who also died as they would
- His victory over death and promises them the victor's crown of life
- He is aware of their situation
- He knows their current condition, but reveals a Kingdom reality—you are rich
- the truth about the deceivers being agents of Satan
- their future suffering spurred by Satan
- the duration of the testing and suffering (like the Babylonian captivity of 70 years)
- that death waits them (but),
- the reward on the other side of the suffering—the crown of life
- the second death will not hurt them

What courage this must have given the Smyrna church! I believe the *Book of Job* would read much differently if Job had known, from the beginning, the source of his afflictions. If I were to write a title for *Job*, it would be, *Job: A Man in Trial without a Word from God*. Job fluctuates from thinking God is against him to knowing he is blameless. How different Job's story would have been had he have known that the source of his affliction was actually the devil! What if Job had also known the promise that awaited him on the other side of his affliction? When we have God's perspective and a waiting promise, the view completely changes. Hearing from God is vital!

Some years ago, in a vision, the Lord showed me a dirt road ascending a hill. As I watched the vision the Holy Spirit said, "Ascend." In the vision, I looked up the parched thirsty dirt road, then glanced down off to my right where there was a very nice stream surrounded by lush green vegetation and shade. I saw that many of my friends were by the stream; they were having a great time laughing and enjoying themselves. I said to the Lord, "I want to go over there with them." He responded, "It will be hard. You will be thirsty and hot, but when you get to the top you will see My Kingdom more clearly." Then He added, "The end of a matter is better than its beginning." Well, that day was the beginning of a journey, which was exactly as the dirt road depicted. The Lord was kind to show me the season I was entering beforehand, but it was, nevertheless, still a very difficult season. The vision He showed me helped me persevere up that dusty dirt road with understanding of my season. He did not speak to me much during those thirsty years, but when He did speak, it was monumental and life-changing. As the Lord and I journeyed up that parched lonely road together, He transformed my understanding of His Kingdom.

Snap shots of prophetic-produced perseverance are throughout the Bible, both in the New Testament and the Old Testament. The prophetic producing perseverance in the people of God is still one of God's intended purposes for the prophetic gifts today.

Topic for discussion:

Discuss examples from scripture (or from personal experience) where God used a prophetic revelation to produce perseverance in His people, or where the prophetic word itself preserved through time and finally came to pass, by finding its intended fulfillment.

Love Never Fails

· ·

17. Love never fails. But where there are prophecies, they will cease; where there are tongues, they will be stilled; where there is knowledge, it will pass away.
Read Matthew 22:36–40, Romans 13:8–10, and Galatians 5:6

Look up the Greek word "πιπτω" (pipto), which is translated "fails" and write its meaning.

In view of the definition of "fails" and the listed scriptures above, what should our aim be?

Romans 13:10 says, "Love does no harm to its neighbor" Relate this to the prophetic.

Love never fails. Prophecies will be fulfilled and the gift of prophecy will end, love however, is eternal; "God is Love." (1 John 4:8) Many prophecies have found their fulfillment and resting place; they ended. Love will never end.

Certain scriptures by definition are fundamental bedrock scriptures. They have words like "all," "only," "first," and "never"; 1 Corinthians 13:8a, Galatians 5:6 and Matthew 22:36–40 are such scriptures. Loving God and His people should be our aim. Jesus, when asked about the greatest commandment stated it is to love God and people (Matthew 22). Also, according to Romans 13:9–10, all the commandments find their embodiment in "Love your neighbor as yourself." Love never fails—(πιπτω) it never descends to a lower place—if it did it would no longer be love. All ministries are at their best when they flow from love's spring. Everything will be better when we put loving God and loving people in its proper place—first!

Consider the placement of 1 Corinthians 13 (the love chapter), again. Both the proceeding and succeeding scriptures to 1 Corinthians 13 give strong attitude mandates towards spiritual gifts, using words like "eagerly desire," which in the Greek is more conclusively, "to burn with zeal." Following 1 Corinthians 12:31 "to burn with zeal" for spiritual gifts, Paul, as if digressing to spotlight another very important thought says (paraphrased), "Let me show you a more excellent way—that is, to pursue spiritual gifts and burn with zeal for them (12:31) *because of love*." Paul's thoughts continue, "In addition, here is what love looks like, acts like, and thinks like (13). So, run after this love (14:1) in order to have the proper heart while burning with zeal for spiritual gifts."

Although love is the focus, it is not the only object in view of the lens. Spiritual gifts are the setting—love is the focal point. People who walk in love desire spiritual gifts because spiritual gifts edify, build, and do good to and for others. People who pursue spiritual gifts without the proper heart of love usually self-destruct spiritually, or because of wrong motivation, carelessly injure others. Moreover, they often end up behind the spiritual woodshed.

Though love is our goal, we will all make mistakes. None of us is perfect in what we say. If we were, according to James 3:2, we would be a perfect man. I was taught and accepted that man could become perfect as a young believer. That was over 33 years ago, and I do not believe it anymore, at least not the way I did back then. Christians are perfectly without the penalty of sin and in perfectly right standing with God, but to be perfect is not possible this side of eternity. Making right choices and living in step with the Holy Spirit, is possible, but perfect— not a chance. Two experiences with the love of God have radically changed my perspective on perfection—God manifested Himself to me as Love. As if He stepped out from behind the veil of eternity for a split second, revealed Himself to me as absolutely pure, flowing, translucent Love and then stepped back behind eternity's veil. In that moment of time, I encountered a Love that is so pure we have not the words to describe, only God Himself can reveal it—since that Love, is God Himself. Meeting Him as pure Love thoroughly changed my opinion as to the ability of man to ever walk in that kind of Love. Someday, we will meet Him face to face, and we will be changed to be like Him. However, while man is in the flesh, man is *in the flesh*.

Selah. Rest here for a little while. Reflect on God and His love toward humanity and you as an individual. I pray you have an encounter with Him behind eternity's veil.

77

• •

18. For we know in part and we prophesy in part,
Matthew 2, 1 Peter 1:10-12, and 2 Peter 1:19–21

Explain, "For we know in part and we prophesy in part" in view of the above scriptures.

What do these scriptures reveal about working together and honoring others' gifts?

The birth of Jesus Christ recorded in Matthew 2 pinpoints just a few of the numerous prophecies fulfilled during the time surrounding Jesus' birth. All the prophets knew in part. However, their many prophecies when stitched together created the tapestry of Jesus' birth, beautifully woven, as the Holy Spirit moved upon different individuals, in different places, and at different times.

Even though the scriptures studied in this section show the many prophecies spoken about the birth of Jesus Christ, "For we know in part and we prophesy in part" has application for prophetic people today. Many local churches have been handicapped (some crippled, some destroyed) because people have lacked the humility and wisdom it takes to work together. When we honor each other's ability to hear the Holy Spirit and pray over the various prophetic revelations, we see they resemble pieces of a puzzle or the blueprint of a construction project. As we team together, the Holy Spirit reveals how each piece fits together forming the complete picture of His revelation: God's purposes, plans, and vision. Whether in a local church, a personal life, or the Church in general, this is true. By God's divine sovereignty, if we are hearing from the Holy Spirit, then somehow all of the separate revelations (however they manifest) together landscape His beautiful architectural plan. Building with God and His people requires humility and understanding.

The prophecy of the dry bones in Ezekiel 37 scrolled through my mind, and as it did, the Lord gave me the interpretation. He said our church had many unfulfilled prophecies; in fact, they (the prophecies) were a valley of dry bones. However, God said if we would pray and fast over the prophecies then He would bring people to fulfill them. He would breathe life into the prophecies and they would come alive. The prophecies were all a part of each other. God would attach them to each other with sinews, flesh, and skin—people. Life would come into them and they would create an exceedingly great army. Prayer and fasting was the key to the fulfillment of the prophecies.

Piecing of prophecies together is also prevalent in end-time events. As we Christians study end-time scriptures, we are like the prophets of old as they searched out the birth and death of Messiah; instead, we are searching out the end-time events. 1 Peter 1:10–11 says, "Concerning this salvation, the prophets, who spoke of the grace that was to come to you, searched intently and with the greatest care, trying to find out the time and circumstances to which the Spirit of Christ in them was pointing when he predicted the sufferings of Christ and the glories that would follow." Many people diligently search out end-time scriptures, trying to piece them together in order to find out "what manner of time" the prophets spoke about in the scriptures. No amount of piecing will unveil what God has sealed: God has sealed Daniel's prophecy until the end (Daniel 12:9), just as the voices of the thunders in *Revelation* are sealed (Revelation 10:4). My husband had a dream years ago; in this dream, he was in the middle of the *Book of Revelation's* fulfillment. Some of the events in *The Book of Revelation* had just happened, and as he looked back at them, it was obvious how they lined up in scripture. However, there was no way to figure them out looking forward. Understanding has to be through revelation by the Holy Spirit and in His timing—man just cannot figure out the things of God, He must reveal them.

"The Spirit searches all things, even the deep things of God." (1 Corinthians 2:10b)

● ●

19. ...but when perfection comes, the imperfect disappears.

How can this scripture help encourage us when we feel like we have given less than the perfect word of prophecy?

SNOW ZONE
CHAINS OR TRACTION TIRES REQUIRED

Read Romans 8:28-39 aloud in first person. Write down anything the Holy Spirit emphasizes to you as you read.

For example, 28 And [I] ~~we~~ know that in all things God works for [my] good ~~of those who~~ [because I] love Him, ~~who~~ [I who] have been called according to His purpose...

Maturing in the prophetic can be a difficult road to travel. It is full of rough terrain and obstacles, many bumps, and bruises will accompany those who brave its trials. Many give up. Why do I talk like this about "but when perfection comes, the imperfect disappears"? Because all of us who have prophetic ministries to one degree or another will at times, feel like we are bloodied and lying on the side of the road; the cause, either friendly fire or more than likely, self-inflicted wounds. Self-inflicted wounds—is that a puzzled look? If we are puzzled at this, then we probably have not much experience in the prophetic. Out of immaturity, we have all probably run ahead of God, said too much, or have not yet realized the spiritual battle, which accompanies those who speak for God through prophetic gifts. (There is more on this subject in Chapter 3, Struggles in the Prophetic.)

2 Corinthians 3:18 says, "But we all, with unveiled face, beholding as in a mirror the glory of the Lord, are being transformed into the same image from glory to glory, just as by the Spirit of the Lord." As we walk with the Lord and exercise our spiritual gifts, we are growing and being transformed. The Lord knew we would not hit the target every time, but He chose to use us anyway. The Lord is very good at making all things work for our good (even our mistakes, bumps, and bruises). Learn from the errors, lick the wounds (just not for too long), and get back up and prophesy again!

As has already been discussed, there are times when we accurately hear a revelation from the Holy Spirit, but how we interpret is where we run into problems. Here is a story where that is exactly what I did, and what I learned.

At a meeting, a pastor asked me to pray for a woman whom I had never met. She did not tell me anything about why she wanted prayer; I just waited to see if God would reveal anything. I laid hands on her, then after a short time, I saw in my spirit "a brain." I interpreted this as a "thought problem" and began to pray for her thought life, praying she would take every thought captive to obey Christ and other related prayers. I did not ask the Lord what the interpretation was for "the brain," which I may add, would have been a very wise thing to ask Him. Come to find out it was not her thought life at all. She had had five brain surgeries, now scheduled for her sixth and last. Spinal fluid was leaking from her brain somewhere near where her head and spine met. The doctors could not stop the leak. God's intent in showing me the brain was to give a word of knowledge to increase both my faith and the woman's faith, resulting in her healing. I did not pause to ask the Holy Spirit what He meant in showing me the brain. What a powerfully sad lesson I learned, too bad the price was so high. Say only what you know. Since I did not know the interpretation, I should have just said, "The Holy Spirit just showed me a brain, does this mean anything to you?"

However, we should not be too hard on ourselves either. We are not perfect yet! Someday on the other side of eternity's door, we will be. Nevertheless, until that day let us just do our best and keep pressing forward. Our outlook should be the same as Paul's in Philippians 3:13–16, "Not that I have already obtained all this, or have already been made perfect, but I press on to take hold of that for which Christ Jesus took hold of me. Brothers, I do not consider myself yet to have taken hold of it. But one thing I do: Forgetting what is behind and straining towards what is ahead, I press on towards the goal to win the prize for which God has called me heavenwards in Christ Jesus. All of us who are mature should take such a view of things. And if on some point you think differently, that too God will make clear to you. Only let us live up to what we have already attained."

When I Was a Child

20. When I was a child, I talked like a child, I thought like a child, I reasoned like a child. When I became a man, I put childish ways behind me.
Jeremiah 23:21–22, 2 Samuel 18:19–33, and 2 Chronicles 30:6–12,

CAUTION CHILDREN

1. How does a child talk, think and reason?

2. How are runners carrying their messages like prophetic people with a message?

3. How does Ahimaaz's childlike immaturity relate to the prophetic today?

4. What does God say in Jeremiah 23 is necessary to carry the word of the Lord?

5. According to Ephesians 4:11–15, what are the characteristic of children, and the mark of maturity?

Standing in the counsel of the Lord is the prerequisite for running with His word. Anyone can recite scriptures and dig up memories from the graveyard of "Remember when God..." But, to be a herald of the fresh wind of His Spirit takes standing in His counsel—in His presence.

Usually, but not always, the more God can trust us, the more He will speak to us for the prophetic. "The Lord confides in those who fear him; he makes his covenant known to them." (Psalm 25:14) We want God to confide in us, we want to run with His word. We want to be a relevant voice in our generation and not just an echo. John the Baptist said, "I am the voice of one calling in the desert, 'Make straight the way for the Lord.'" Too many people become an echo, only faintly resembling someone else's voice. Stand in His counsel. Be a voice.

Runners in the Old Testament are analogous to prophetic people. They ran with messages bringing news, warning, etc., from the king. 2 Chronicles describes runners who ran throughout the country with letters from the king. In these letters, the king commanded his people to repent and return to the Lord, followed by warning if they did not heed his message. This sounds much like the prophetic (especially a prophet) carrying a word from our King.

Ahimaaz was ambitious and careless. When he got the *microphone* in his hand, his lack of first hand news was in full display for King David. King David's son Absalom was dead, yet Ahimaaz said to the king, "All is well!" He had no news ready, he had nothing to say, yet he just wanted to say something—anything—foolish Ahimaaz! He had not seen what took place: the king's son was dead! Stand aside Ahimaaz; let me give the *microphone* to someone who has first hand news from the Lord, to someone who has stood in His counsel, and to whom God has revealed His secrets.

Sloppy runners ruin their reputation and the reputation of the prophetic gift. "As dead flies give perfume a bad smell, so a little folly outweighs wisdom and honor." (Ecclesiastes 10:1) It is a child who wants to run with every little thing they think God has said to them. Remember hearing is just the first step. Do we really have something God wants us to speak to others? Do not run ahead of God, we will live to regret it! Train in the proper training ground not before the king! Remember to be quick to hear and slow to speak. The flesh can *drive* us to be impulsive, but the Holy Spirit will *lead* us in the will of God. Let us not give into the impulsion of our flesh. Instead, as we humble ourselves, God will exalt us in due time.

When I was a child, I talked, thought, and reasoned like a child. [However] when I became a man, I put childish ways behind me. Children are careless with their words and behavior, believe whatever they are told, and reason through self-interest, emotion, and short-term (need or want based) thinking. Jesus gives the 5-fold ministers to equip the saints for the work of ministry, to build up the body of Christ [until His return]; *so that* the church will grow up to maturity *by speaking the truth in love*, and will no longer be swayed by deceptive teaching, as a child would. Speaking the truth in love is the *very heart* of the prophetic.

> SPEAKING THE TRUTH IN LOVE IS THE VERY HEART OF THE PROPHETIC.

If you ran ahead of God and now find yourself feeling perhaps like Ahimaaz felt, whether out of zeal for spiritual gifts or due to a lack of wisdom, then let the Holy Spirit's discipline have its appropriate work in you. God's purpose for disciplining us is so that we will better next time we prophesy, not to humiliate us into quitting. Let us learn our lessons well, so we do not have to take another lap around the spiritual woodshed. Press on—earnestly desiring spiritual gifts—especially the gift of prophecy!

Now I Know in Part

21. Now we see but a poor reflection as in a mirror; then we shall see face to face. Now I know in part; then I shall know fully, even as I am fully known.
Matthew 6:22–23, 13:10–17, 2 Corinthians 3:18, and 1 John 3:2–3

Why does God still speak in parables, dreams, and visions today?

How does the clarity of our own "eye" affect our spiritual perspective and vision?

Limitations we face while in the body verses the clarity of understanding we will have when we see Him Face to face is central to this scripture. While we live in the flesh, we will struggle with the flesh and our natural confines and understanding. However, when we see Him Face to face, *then* we shall know fully even as we are fully known. Consequently, this is the reason it can be easy to misunderstand what God is communicating to us through parables, pictures, dreams, vision, and other revelatory gifts.

Jesus deliberately spoke in parables so people would turn to Him (Matthew 13 loosely paraphrased). Many times Jesus' own disciples did not understand Him and asked for explanations. (Their interaction is often humorous.) Parables, pictures, dreams, and visions still cause the human heart to stay in close relationship with the Lord for understanding and interpretation. He does not want a textbook relationship with His people. Even after Jesus told the disciples, "The knowledge of the secrets of the kingdom of heaven has been given to you, but not to them" (Matthew 13:11), the disciples still had many questions and still did not understand much of what Jesus said to them. In 2 Peter 3:16, Peter writes concerning the Apostle Paul, "His letters contain some things that are hard to understand, which ignorant and unstable people distort, as they do the other Scriptures, to their own destruction." Even the Apostle Peter had a hard time understanding what the Holy Spirit spoke through Paul.

Think about all the accounts of dreams people had in the Bible. Many times God interpreted the dream Himself, while other times He sent an interpreter. Dreams, where another interprets, cause believers to work together, much like tongues and interpretation. In the cases of Pharaoh and Joseph, or Nebuchadnezzar and Daniel, God used hidden messages in dreams to reveal Himself to a godless man and nation. The Holy Spirit, who is the revealer of mysteries, interprets dreams. If we want more clarity and the foggy reflection to clear, it takes seeking the Lord. The answers come along with the relationship. As we develop an ongoing personal relationship with the Holy Spirit, He works together with us to purify our hearts; we will then see the things of God more clearly and our part in them. The vision, plans, and purposes God has in His heart for us will become clearer to us.

1 Corinthians 13:12 reminds me of a lake in Central Oregon named Clear Lake. It is a fascinating lake because of its clarity. Clear Lake, fed primarily by snow runoff is from nearby Mount Washington and the surrounding areas. The runoff filters through underground caverns for more than 20 years before emptying into Clear Lake. Clear Lake forms the headwaters of the McKenzie River, which flows out of its southern end, flowing near Eugene, Oregon, into the Willamette River and on to the Pacific Ocean. Clear Lake has visibility to nearly 200 feet deep! (en.wikipedia.org/wiki/Clear_Lake_(Linn_County,_Oregon) Compare this to a little tadpole pond full of salamanders and algae. Clarity is much greater when we look through something, which is clean and pure. Our perception and ability to hear the Holy Spirit speak is connected to the singleness of our eyes; the cleanness of our own hearts and minds, and is so vital. What we set our affections on guides the course of our lives. If we truly want to hear the Holy Spirit, we must keep our eyes healthy (Matthew 6:22–23).

Topic for discussion:

Compare Numbers 21:8–9, 2 Kings 18:4, John 3:14 and Revelation 12:9: Why is it important to hear the interpretation from the Holy Spirit instead of using a methodized interpretation system?

◆ ◆

22. And now these three remain: faith, hope, and love. But the greatest of these is love.

In view of the prophetic what is this scripture saying?

Read Revelation 2 and 3 and then identify how Jesus' words to each church would increase their faith, give them hope, and display to them the love of God.

God's intent for the prophetic is to deposit faith, hope, and love into the hearts of the intended hearers:

- Faith: The prophetic word will increase the faith of the hearer or hearers. Whether, by the Holy Spirit, the revelation reveals the secrets of someone's heart, reveals the future, encourages the faint hearted, or gives hope in a desperate situation, the hearers' faith increases when the prophetic word is given.

- Hope: Hope deposited into the hearers will increase their expectation in God. It awakens the heart in such a way that we realize God is aware of us and cares for us. The prophetic has encouraged the faint-hearted; many hopeless, weak, fearful warriors have had renewed vigor through the prophetic. Many times, God reveals what is ahead for his beloved people in order that they may look back on a word spoken to them and have hope in and beyond their current situation.

- Love: Love is always the backdrop for anything God speaks through a prophetic revelation. Anything God reveals is because He loves and *is* love. God loves people and the prophetic, whether directly or indirectly, will reveal His loving heart. When we hear a word from the Lord that speaks to our situation, it gives us courage to press on, forging ahead, realizing afresh that God is with us and loves us, though the road is difficult. So then, we who speak for God as His mouthpiece must flow in and through love, accurately presenting the prophetic as God intends. Our presentation, attitude, passion, voice fluctuation, and volume, must embody—speaking the truth in love.

The greatest of these is love.

Looking at the prophetic love-letters to the seven churches in *Revelation,* we can see that Jesus is imparting faith, hope, and love in each letter. Jesus builds each church's faith by statements showing He knows each church personally, their struggles, sins, and victories. Jesus does not leave the people without hope. He tells each church what they must do in order to keep their lampstand. Jesus also speaks of the promises awaiting them if they overcome. He spoke truth to each church exactly as they needed to hear it, giving each an opportunity to repent where needed—that is love. Jesus identifies Himself individually to each church depending upon what they were facing. For example, to Smyrna He identifies Himself as "the One Who was dead and is now alive," knowing they would soon face death themselves. Each letter in the *Book of Revelation* reveals Jesus' obvious love towards the churches individually scripted depending upon what each faced.

Topic for discussion:

Brainstorm over prophecies in the Bible, can you identify in them the concept of faith, hope, and love?

Conclusion

◆ ◆

The Heart of the Prophetic

1 Corinthians 12:31 began our excavation into the Heart of the Prophetic:
"But eagerly desire the greater gifts. And now I will show you the most excellent way."

Excavating the "more excellent way," we uncovered the wealth of treasure God had for us in 1 Corinthians 13, keeping it in context as it is found in the Bible: sandwiched between 1 Corinthians 12 and 1 Corinthians 14. 1 Corinthians 12 ends with a discussion on spiritual gifts and the passion with which we are to desire them. 1 Corinthians 14 picks up where 1 Corinthians 12 left off, adding the proper attitude and heart with which people are to both manifest and pursue spiritual gifts. 1 Corinthians 13 is the vein of gold interposed between the two. 1 Corinthians 13 is the explanatory heart, fusing 1 Corinthians 12:31 to 1 Corinthians 14:1.

1 Corinthians 12:31 → 1 Corinthians 13 ← 1 Corinthians 14:1

Some have erroneously mishandled these scriptures in 1 Corinthians 13, arguing that love replaces spiritual gifts. When in truth, love is to be the culture for spiritual gifts. Loving others means we will pursue spiritual gifts in order to build up the body of Christ, edifying each other. It is through this avenue the body of Christ matures, and is able to stand against the winds of doctrines, which try to blow her off course and into error. Speaking the truth in love is both at the heart of the prophetic and the maturing of the church.

If the Greek definitions were added 1 Corinthians 14:1 would read as follows:

> Pursue love. That is, run swiftly after making sure to catch and acquire love—make love your aim. Both press on towards love and follow after love, and as you do, burn with zeal in hot pursuit of spiritual gifts. Yes, strive after and busy yourself in the acquiring of spiritual gifts—the best gifts. As you busy yourself in the acquiring of spiritual gifts, exert yourself especially to building others up through prophesy.

Chapter 3

•••

Struggles in the Prophetic

Submit yourselves, then, to God.
Resist the devil, and he will flee from you.
James 4:7

For our struggle is not against flesh and blood, but against the
rulers, against the authorities, against the powers of this dark
world and against the spiritual forces of evil in the heavenly realms.
Ephesians 6:12

He [Jesus] replied, "I saw Satan fall like lightning from heaven.
I have given you authority to trample on snakes and scorpions and
to overcome all the power of the enemy; nothing will harm you.
However, do not rejoice that the spirits submit to you, but rejoice
that your names are written in heaven."
Luke 10:18-20

Introduction

◆ ◆

Struggles in the Prophetic

N O LIGHTNING BOLTS, NO EXPLOSIONS, NO FIREWORKS... Earlier in the day, God had given me a prophecy, but now I was suffering under the weight of an allusive, gloomy condemnation. It was dominating every thought and emotion within me. A deep darkness would settle over me, robbing every ounce of joy I should have experienced after giving a prophecy. As I sat under that miserable dark cloud, a thought popped into my mind, *Could this be a spirit of condemnation?* "In the Name of Jesus, I rebuke you, spirit of condemnation," I said. At the time it did not seem like much happened. No lightning bolts, no explosions, no fireworks—just that dark cloud blew away. In that seemingly uneventful afternoon, the Lord gave me understanding that transformed my ability to hold up under the enemy's attacks.

A couple weeks ago, I stayed with a young woman to help her move. I slept in her bed while she slept on the floor next to me. As I was about to fall asleep, panic suddenly flooded, my mind and my heart began to race. Wondering if it was a demon, under my breath, I rebuked the spirit in the Name of Jesus. It was gone! 10 seconds later—BAM—the panic came surging back with intensity, my heart rapidly racing, and the panic attack, severe. Now, sure it was a demon, in the Name of Jesus, I rebuked the spirit and had instant peace. Careless demon, its lies were exposed; it assumed I was the young woman. For years, this young woman suffered anxiety and panic attacks. She had turned to prescription medication for help, especially for sleeping. Whether or not it began with a demon or whether the demon was just taking an opportunity through a weakness, we do not know, but we do know it was exploiting the situation. Now, brought into the light, we dealt with it in the Name of Jesus!

Any little cracked door is an invitation to the enemy, and he will slither through any way he can. His goal is death and chaos in our lives. We all have gifts and talents given to us by the Holy Spirit, and as we walk with the Lord to accomplish what He has for us, the enemy lurks to stop us, if he can. Despite the fact that we are always in war, often by the Lord's sovereignty, we are not privy to the enemies' attacks. Other times God allows us to see the reality of our battle. It is in these times God often speaks to us through the exploits of King David, the shepherd warrior; or Gideon, the apprehensive warrior; or Abraham, the faith warrior. Some of us have never been at war, but God has taught us to war spiritually as others fought physically. When we set out to accomplish the plans the Lord has for us, we will encounter enemies, real enemies, though usually unseen by the physical eye. They plot, they plan, and they strategize how to take us down. Do not be outwitted by their schemes.

Struggles in the Prophetic, written with war in mind, purposefully visits certain scriptures leading to the spiritual weapons cache. As you study, acquire your spiritual weapons.

Shutting Open Doors

Samson: Anointing Without Character

1. Read Judges chapters 13–15
    How would you describe Samson's character?

2. Read Judges 16
    a. Briefly summarize this chapter.

    b. Which two scriptures stick out the most to you?

    c. Which New Testament scripture(s) comes to mind as you reflect on Samson's life?

    d. Whom does Delia resemble?

    e. What were her tactics?

Wisdom and knowledge each have their beginning in the fear of God; (Proverbs 1:7 and 9:10) Samson's lack of character reveals he is void of both. Many pejoratives come to mind when pondering Samson—a loose cannon, an immoral mindless brute, stupid—boorish. He taunted the Philistines, enticing them to anger with his arrogance and flippant attitude. Interestingly, scripture does not mention God interacting with Samson. God answers Samson's prayers, yet there is not relationship-communications between the two. It appears Samson did all this "on his own," using God's gift and anointing instead of *it* using him. Romans 12:19 states vengeance belongs to God, but Samson thought it was his. However, God was seeking an occasion against the Philistines and used Samson in spite of him. God's gifts and callings are irrevocable (Romans 11:29), which reveals why someone living in sin or who has left God can still operate in their gifts, and even be anointed for a time. Never be impressed by anointing, rather be impressed by the character of Jesus you see in someone's life (Rodney Howard-Browne). God used someone like Samson, how much more will He use a heart that belongs to Him?

Judges 14:2 exposes Samson's enormous character liability. Samson's lust for ungodly women was his demise. He demanded, "Go get her for me" though she was a nameless Philistine. He showed no regard for the law of God, acting unlawfully by marrying a heathen. Samson's first mistake was that he allowed his heart to go after Nameless Philistine; next, he was with her, walking right into temptation, and finally he married her. Sin is progressive—it does not stop until it has killed. Genesis 4:7 states it this way, "sin is crouching at your door; it desires to have you, but you must master it." The Hebrew for "master" is to rule, have dominion, to reign. Walking and living by the Holy Spirit is the only way to master sin. Galatians 5:16, "So I say, live by the Spirit, and you will not gratify the desires of the sinful nature." Get dominion over sin, through walking and living by the Holy Spirit, before it kills you.

Women were an obvious weakness to Samson. Judges 16 again sets Samson's boorishness on display for all to see. He goes after another unlawful ungodly woman, Delilah. She, too, is a tool in the enemies' hands. Delilah and his first wife (Nameless) used the same exact tactics. Samson should have wised up after Nameless, he should have known better. Repeatedly, he uses the anointing instead of the anointing using him. Samson is reckless, thoughtless, and easily manipulated—*from the inside out*. Interesting how the enemy works. Samson again willingly gives into pressure from the enemy, playing games by the anointing of God.

Delilah resembles the flesh or the sinful earthy nature. When we give into it, it will weaken and ultimately kill us. Samson was under assault by the "hidden guys." (Judges 16:9-12) They used the flesh (Delilah), as a pawn, to find Samson's weakness to ruin him. All the while, promising the flesh (Delilah) it would benefit. The "hidden guys" resemble demons—they work in secret hiding behind closed doors. They tempt, they wait, they ponder, they observe, they watch. Then, when a weakness manifests, they try to bring death (spiritual or natural) through it.

Sin can be pleasurable (Hebrews 11:25 and Genesis 3:6); otherwise, it would not be temptation. James 1:13 states, "When tempted, no one should say, 'God is tempting me.' For God cannot be tempted by evil, nor does he tempt anyone." Delilah was only the tool or vehicle Samson's enemies used to try to destroy him. Samson saw Delilah as desirable. Yet, she had secret intent to kill him, spurred on by the Philistines, the enemies of God. We are supposed to put to death whatever belongs to our earthy nature (Colossians 3:5), not entertain it. Delilah resembles the way the flesh operates if we do not put it to death. It nags; it leads us into spiritual lethargy, spurred on by the enemies hiding behind closed doors. If we entertain the lust of the flesh, we will die in one way or another. Delilah used ridicule, emotionalism (you do not love me), lethargy (she lured him to sleep), she nagged and pestered him, she covenanted with him in marriage. She exploited him by preying on his weaknesses.

Heart-wrenching scriptures: (Samson, awaken from your death-gripping lullaby!)
- "With such nagging she prodded him day after day until he was sick to death of it. So he told her everything." (Judges 16:16–17)
- "After putting him to sleep on her lap, she called for someone to shave off the seven braids of his hair, and so began to subdue him. And his strength left him. Then she called, 'Samson, the Philistines are upon you!' He awoke from his sleep and thought, 'I'll go out as before and shake myself free.' But he did not know that the Lord had left him." (Judges 16:19–20)

Consider all consequences following Samson giving into the lust of the flesh. Samson repeatedly broke the covenant God had with Israel. However, like Pharaoh with Moses, God uses everything for His purposes, "For the Scripture says to Pharaoh: 'I raised you up for this very purpose, that I might display my power in you and that my name might be proclaimed in all the earth.'" (Romans 9:17) God ultimately used Samson for His purposes, but it cost him the anointing and in the end—his life.

Samson was so stupid! Did he not wonder why Delilah kept trying to find the secret of his strength? Every time he told her his weakness, she would test it—she was a Philistine! Samson, on the edge, fell over. Delilah and Nameless weakened him day by day, not right away. Ever so slowly, the temptation became more and more familiar, and he recognized it less and less. Instead of killing the lust within, Samson made a peace treaty with it, and it ruined him.

"...but each one is tempted when, by his own evil desire, he is dragged away and enticed. Then, after desire has conceived, it gives birth to sin; and sin, when it is full-grown, gives birth to death. Don't be deceived, my dear brothers." (James 1:14–16) Samson's story is a reminder to us to put to death the works of the sinful nature instead of trying to live with them, to control our thought life, turn off bad TV, and not look again at the immodestly dressed. Over time, temptations get more and more deadly, but we recognize them less and less. If temptation is not mastered, like the cute baby tiger that comes to live in our basement, it will grow, and in the end maim or kill us. We begin to accept things we would have been appalled at years earlier. Duller and duller we become, opening a door for the enemy, a door that used to be nonexistent. Though God does not leave us, the precious anointing we once walked in, ever so slowly does. Do not walk on the edge; rather say as Jesus did, "sin has no part in Me."

Samson's story could have been about redemption and victory had he conquered his lust for foreign women and stopped playing games with the enemy—if he would have learned his lessons and gained a heart of wisdom. Our story can be one of redemption and victory, even if we have lived as Samson did. Walk and live by the Holy Spirit and you will not gratify the desires of the sinful nature. In relationship with the Holy Spirit, we can shut all our open doors.

SCENIC BYWAY

Personal:

Take some time to consider your own life. Is the Lord is speaking to you about any open doors?

Discouragement

◆ ◆

Elijah: A Man Like Us

1. Read James 5:17–18, 1 Kings 17:1–5 and 1 Kings 18
   Describe Elijah and briefly summarize these scriptures.

2. Read 1 Kings 19
   a. Describe Elijah in this chapter.

   b. What caused such a drastic contrast in Elijah compared to chapters 17 and 18?

   c. What were Jezebel's tactics?

   d. Whom does Jezebel resemble and how?

   e. How does God respond to Elijah in chapter 19?

There are a number of prominent people in the Bible and Elijah is one of them. His life is full of the mighty exploits of the Old Testament prophets, and yet James 5:17 states, "Elijah was a man just like us" with emotional vacillations, fears and victories, bravery and retreats. 1 Kings 18 is one of Elijah's finest moments, juxtaposed to 1 Kings 19, which pins up Elijah's weakness for us all to see. Somewhere in Elijah's life story, we will all probably read about ourselves. Allow God to use Elijah's life to work in each of us, to retool, reshape,—re-vision us. Let us learn to set aside our emotions and natural understanding to the truth of God's absolute sovereignty.

"At the time of the offering of the evening sacrifice, Elijah the prophet came near and said, 'O Lord, the God of Abraham, Isaac and Israel, today let it be known that you are God in Israel and that I am your servant and I have done all these things at your word.'" (1 Kings 18:36 NAS) An interesting choice of words, "At the time of the offering of the evening sacrifice, Elijah the prophet *came near* and said." Elijah *came near*—to where? He was already at the altar, he had just poured water all over it, but now he *came near*—to God. Verse 36 goes on to say, "...and said, 'Lord.'" The NIV is the only version of the nine I looked at which says Elijah *stepped* forward. The Hebrew literally means, "to draw near, approach." It is the same word used in Jeremiah 30:21 (NAS) "'...and he shall *approach* Me; For who would dare to risk his life to *approach* Me?' declares the LORD." The time of the evening sacrifice was 3:00 in the afternoon. Think back on all the activity that had already taken place earlier in the day. If Elijah had left after he had put the water on the altar, then it would have seeped into the soil. Since he was already at the altar, it seems he could not have drawn near it. Elijah was a man close to God; he knew how to draw near to Him, to hear His voice.

Elijah had God's Glory in mind, "...let it be known this day that you are God." Elijah was not trying to bring attention to himself he pointed to God, "I am your servant." Elijah makes it clear the voice of God was his guide, "I have done all these things at your word." His purpose was to bring back the hearts of the people to the Lord.

Elijah lived in obedience to God's voice. Ahab, the wicked king, knew him as a troubler of Israel, Elijah turned the whole nation of Israel back to God, and he killed the 450 prophets of Baal. Elijah heard and saw things in the spiritual realm. He was a man of persistent prayer, he recognized the hand of God when it was only faintly noticeable on the horizon, he gave direction to Ahab, and God moved him beyond natural human ability.

What happened to drastically change this Elijah we read about in chapter 18, to the Elijah of Chapter 19? Elijah sounds depressed in 1 Kings 19:4–7; he wants to die, and is just eating and sleeping (howbeit supernaturally). Was Elijah really the only one left? God said He had reserved 7000 who had not bowed the knee to Baal. If "they" really were seeking his life in verse 10, was not God the same God who had just used Elijah to put to death the 450 Baal prophets. What changed? Elijah received a threatening message from an evil woman (Jezebel), and he believed it. Even though Jezebel lied, by believing what she said, Elijah's perspective changed, instantaneously from faith to fear. During one of our small group discussions, a man questioned, "what if all those prophets of Baal were demon possessed or at least demon harassed? What happened to all of the demons when Elijah put their Baal prophet hosts to death?" (Remember the demons and the pigs in Matthew 8.) It is possible the demons, which were deceiving Baal's dead prophets, were now attacking Elijah. Elijah became fearful, depressed, and despondent; he wanted to die. This sounds like demonic activity. We can also become like Elijah, from faith to fear in an instant, when devilish messengers verbally harass us, and then we believe what they say.

Thank God, through Jesus, we Christians have authority over them! Ephesians 4:17 says the sword of the Spirit is the word (rhema) of God. Jesus spoke the scriptures, in context, by the revelation of God, when He was under the assault of Satan. Know the word. Speak the word.

God fed Elijah supernaturally, giving him strength for his journey to of all places Mount Horeb, the Mountain of God. The very same place Moses met with God. Moses and Elijah both stood on Mount Horeb as the Lord passed by (1 Kings 19:11 & Exodus 33:22). God responds to Elijah in the cave without a rebuke, instead saying, "Elijah what are you doing here?" David also ran to a cave from Saul, and God did not get angry with him either. It sounds as though God just waited to let Elijah "get it all out" before He spoke to him again saying, "Go back the way you came." Sound familiar? Sometimes that is exactly what God says to us too, in order to get us back on track. Then, as if to say, Oh, by the way Elijah..., "Yet, I reserve 7,000 in Israel—all whose knees have not bowed down to Baal and whose mouths have not kissed him."

Before we leave Elijah, here are a couple personal experiences, where God spoke to me using Elijah's life story.

Clearly, God had led my husband, George, and me to our current location. However, we began to believe He was leading us to make a move. We were having a difficult time deciding what to do, since God had led us there. Would God lead us to one place and then lead to move? The Holy Spirit spoke to me through a video He played in my spirit. It was of Elijah wailing at the Brook Cherith after it dried up. (Of course, this is not exactly, as you read it the Bible; it is how the Lord spoke rhema to me through Elijah's life.) In the vision, Elijah was kneeling down with his hands reaching out to God, mourning and crying—wailing, "God, You led me here and now the Brook has dried up." The Lord said it was not until the Brook dried up that He gave further instructions to Elijah. Furthermore, just because the Brook dried up it does not mean Elijah had not heard from God to begin with; now, it was time to hear for further direction. After the brook dried up, the Lord spoke to Elijah. He told him to go to Zarephath. God had commanded a widow to provide for him there. Elijah had to remain in constant relationship with the Lord, hearing from Him every step of the way, and so do we. When our brook dries up, God will speak direction, again. Mourning the brook hinders our walk. Look forward to meeting the widow.

In chapter 18, Elijah taunts and mocks the Baal prophets. When mocking demons as a young Christian, it did not go well for me, either. We lived on a mountain in a rural community outside Corvallis, Oregon, and I was home alone often. The closest house was nearly a quarter mile away through a densely treed forest. Praying two hours a day, I had a deep, vital relationship with the Lord. However, I became quite ignorantly flippant about the enemy, taunting and mocking him saying, "Hey devil! Did you know Jesus Christ died for my sins! All authority is Jesus', hum... That means you do not have any!" And etcetera. A very terrifying, intense, dark presence soon came for a visit every time I prayed. I could no longer sleep without fear, waking up in fear, being choked in my sleep, and having very horrifying demonic dreams where I was being hunted by demons. I knew if I could just say the Name of Jesus they would have to leave, but they choked me and I could not speak. I do not have all the answers for the questions this kind of experience surfaces. I however, did learn a great lesson through it from Jude. When Michael the archangel was contending with the devil about the body of Moses, he did not bring against him a reviling accusation, but said, "The Lord rebuke you!" I believe the Lord allowed the enemy access to me, howbeit on a tether, to teach me a lesson. (1 Timothy 1:20) Jesus did not go around hunting for demons or taunting the devil.

Jesus instead dealt with the devil/demons when He encountered them. Elijah taunted the prophets of Baal, too, and hence the spirits accompanying them. His resulting experience was not much different from mine. Focus on Jesus Christ. Deal with the enemy when confronted by him. The enemy wants attention; do not give it to him needlessly.

In conclusion, years ago I heard an apostolic leader of a very large family of churches preach on discouragement. He said all his years of experience had taught him that discouragement was the most prevalent reason pastors quit the ministry. Another pastor told me he had gone back to school to get his PhD after a divorce and resignation from the ministry. He was writing his dissertation on, none other than, discouragement. He saw the root of his collapse was discouragement.

Discouragement can set in ever so quietly, ever so subtlety. It slowly wraps a noose around the neck of its victim, strangling life and vision in its clutches. The prey becomes disillusioned with God and life in general. Discouragement speaks words of enticement, "Come try this it will fulfill you," or it will slither in words of doubt as with John the Baptist in the prison cell, "Is He really the One?" We have all been discouraged from time to time, some survive,—some do not. If this is fitting for you, open up to someone who is trustworthy, and full of the Spirit of God; someone who will stand by you and speak words of life to you. Most of all, tell God everything, and if words flee, sit in His presence and cry if you must. This season will pass and brighter days will come. Find some promises in Bible that are pertinent to your situation; write them down, read them, pray them, confess them, memorize them; have them continually in your thoughts. Use them as weapons. Use them for the comfort that comes from the scriptures. (Romans 15:4)

Topic for discussion:

Did God choose Elisha to replace Elijah as prophet *because* Elijah disqualified himself when he ran from Jezebel in fear?

As we studied Elijah in our small group some people believed he disqualified himself, others (me included) did not.

Things to consider:

Why I do not believe Elijah disqualified himself:
- God doesn't show any anger or judgment
- Elijah does not taste death
- His anointing does not diminish
- Elijah disciples Elisha then passes on his anointing
- He gets fed supernaturally
- Elijah is with Jesus on the Mount of Transfiguration

Why some believe, Elijah did disqualify himself:
- God told him to anoint Elisha to replace him
- Moses was disqualified and he was with Elijah on the Mount of Transfiguration
- Hebrews 11 does not mention Elijah

"Find rest, O my soul, in God alone; my hope comes from him. He alone is my rock and my salvation; he is my fortress, I will not be shaken. My salvation and my honor depend on God; he is my mighty rock, my refuge. Trust in him at all times, O people; pour out your hearts to him, for God is our refuge." (Psalm 62:5–8)

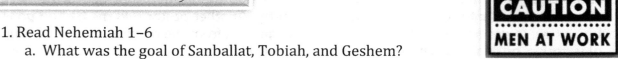

Tools of the Enemy

Sanballat, Tobiah, and Geshem

**CAUTION
MEN AT WORK**

1. Read Nehemiah 1–6
   a. What was the goal of Sanballat, Tobiah, and Geshem?

   b. List the tools used against Nehemiah and the workers (example: Nehemiah 4:1; ridicule).

   c. What parallels are there between the tools Nehemiah's enemies used, trying to stop the work of God, and the devil's tools he uses against the people of God today?

   d. Write your thoughts about Nehemiah 2:10 and 4:1 in view of this section.

Personal Reflection: Take some time to pray specifically about openings in your "wall," where the enemy may be exploiting your weaknesses and using his tools against you. Bring these into the Light; talk to the Lord about them and watch Him rebuild your wall.

Nehemiah was a Jewish exile in Persia, sovereignly placed by God as cup-bearer to King Artaxerxes. Jerusalem and her wall, destroyed by the Babylonians years before, still lay in ruins. Nehemiah, burdened by God, asked permission from the king to go rebuild the city and her walls. King Artaxerxes granted Nehemiah incredible favor. Incomparably important to a city was its wall. It defended the city from invading intruders; soldiers also fought advancing enemies from the wall.

Sanballat, Tobiah, and Geshem's hatred towards the Jews made them determined to stop the rebuilding work to the wall of Jerusalem at any cost. Our enemy also will stop at nothing (except God) to hinder, disrupt and stop the work of God in and through our lives. Nehemiah 2:10 says, "When Sanballat the Horonite and Tobiah the Ammonite official heard about this, they were very much disturbed that someone (literally "adam, a man" [analogous to Jesus Christ, the second Adam, 1 Corinthians 15:45]) had come to promote the welfare of the Israelites." Nehemiah and his dealings with Sanballat, Tobiah, and Geshem reveal a great deal about how our enemy deals with us. Our enemy is indignant and deeply disturbed that God has come to restore our person (and all willing humanity). We may not hear his threats, lies, and intimidation with our natural ears, but they are nonetheless real and can penetrate our hearts, causing fear and retreat if we are not spiritually minded and on our guard. Allow the Holy Spirit to impart wisdom and understanding through the tactics Nehemiah's enemies used against him and then relate them to your life.

Sanballat, Tobiah, and Geshem used every tactic they could, trying to get the rebuilding work to stop. Nevertheless, Nehemiah and the Jews armed up, organized, and trusted in God, and the work continued. Following are some of the tactics Nehemiah's enemies used against him:

Strategies by Enemy
- distraction
- intent to harm
- persistence to wear Nehemiah down
- tried to back Nehemiah into a corner so he would relent and meet with Sanballet and Geshem
- "it will never be completed"
- enemy unites to create confusion
- stirred up opposition
- secret informer sent
- treason with Tobiah—some from Judah secretly communicated with him because they were related and Tobiah used what they said to try and instill fear in Nehemiah
- an evil report
- reproach

Personal Attacks
- mockery
- scoffing
- tried to overwhelm the Jews by making them think the job was too big
- accused of self-serving motivation
- if completed it would be weak and would not stand up to protect the city
- intending to create fear
- their threats and rumors of stealth attacks worked getting into the Jews' mindset and speech, panic set in
- accusation—self-promotion
- accusation—self interest
- accusation—rebellion against authority wanting it for self

Religious Attacks
- said God was not involved
- said God would not be honored
- Shemaiah tries enticing him with religious talk ("Let us meet together in the house of God, within the temple")
- entrapment by false prophesies to cause fear and sin
- using prophets for self advancement
- tries to get Nehemiah to rely on the secret informer for security instead of God even using God's house

Nehemiah has significant insight on spiritual warfare and Holy Spirit led living. Time does not suffice to write about all that we glean by his life. Nehemiah responds in faith, keeps his goal in view, disciplines himself toward that goal, helps others stay focused, receives wisdom, insights, and direction from God along the way; strategizes and organizes the people, recognizes the enemies' tactics, and does not give into fear. He trusts God the whole way through. Incredibly, Jerusalem's wall, 52 days later, was complete!

The Devil

Read Isaiah 14:9-17 and Ezekiel 28:12-19.
1. What is most prominent to you about Satan?

2. Read Rev 12:9–10
   a. What is the devil busy doing and how often?

   b. Look up "devil" and "Satan" in a dictionary; summarize his name and title.

   c. Read Matthew 4:1-11
      1. When did he come to tempt Jesus?

      2. What was the devil's first tactic?

      3. What title does the devil wear in verse 3?

      4. What tactics did the devil use against Jesus?

      5. How did Jesus Respond?

   d. Read Luke 4:13, what does this scripture reveal about your enemy?

Satan wants Jesus' throne and identity. Jesus' identity was the first thing the devil attacked saying, "if you are the Son of God..." Juxtaposing Satan's assertions in Isaiah 14 to the identity of Jesus found in scripture:

Satan's assertion to Jesus' identity

1. "I will ascends to Heaven";
2. "I will raise my throne above the stars of God"; (stars sometimes refer to angles [Revelation 1:20])
3. "I will sit enthroned on the mount of assembly, on the utmost heights of the sacred mountain" (obviously referring to Mount Zion—the Church [Psalm 48:2 and Revelation 14:1]);
4. "I will ascend above the tops of the clouds" (Hebrew root for clouds—also from Ezekiel 28:14);
5. "I will make myself like the Most High." Cults and world religions, want to become God, or/and equal to Him. (Some deny God's existence, which also, is a doctrine of devils.)

Jesus' identity from scripture

1. Jesus ascended to Heaven after He first descended. (Ephesians 4:9-10)
2. Hebrews 1 (especially 1:8 and 1:13) is clear concerning the supremacy of Jesus Christ over all, and in particular, angles.
3. Jesus is the head of the church and stands with His people on Mount Zion, and Zion is the city of God.
4. Jesus is our covering. From Eden, where God first covered our nakedness and sin; to Boaz covering Ruth; to Jesus' ultimate sacrifice providing us covering as our Bridegroom, authority, head of the church—as our all-in-all; Jesus covers us.
5. Jesus is, I AM, the Most High. (John 8:58 and Hebrews 1:8)

Ezekiel 28 reveals Satan's characteristics when God created him, which can shed some light on why Satan is so skilled at deceiving the world. Understanding some of his attributes will help us avoid some of his snares and tactics.

- He was perfect in beauty as created.
- He was full of wisdom.
- His adornments were nine beautiful and precious stones. Interestingly, many of these stones coincide with the foundation of New Jerusalem and the ephod of the high priest.
- Gold workmanship is characteristic of him.
- Isaiah 14:11 and Ezekiel 28:13 reveal the musical and worship characteristics of Lucifer; (enlightening in view of the intense youth movement in music, and much of it is very dark. The devil frequently promotes his doctrine by enticing people through his music. The lyrics regularly promote the world, the flesh, and the devil.)
- He was on the mountain of God—Mount Horeb, where Elijah and Moses met with God.
- He is acquainted with the ways of God, and wisdom and perfection, though now only through corruption and darkness.

In Isaiah 14 and Ezekiel 28, we see much of the antichrist's identity. Additionally, a great deal of the imagery resembles the harlot and the beast she rides in Revelation 17-18.

The devil accuses the people of God day and night. His title "devil" means false accuser, slanderer, and opposer of God. Satan in the Greek Lexicon means "adversary, the inveterate adversary of God and Christ. He incites apostasy from God and to sin." He is a liar. Do not believe him.

Weak, hurting, and lonely people are his prey. Conquering the strong, brilliant, and wise is his trophy. Nothing about him resembles the Lord Jesus in the slightest way. He waited until Jesus was hungry from a complete 40 day fast before he tempted Him with food. Having no mercy, no compassion, and no empathy—he is altogether evil.

Taking the word of God out of context is one of the devil's repetitive deceptions. For centuries, it has worked so he keeps at it. He has built many of the false religions and cults using this approach. They come ever so close to truth, yet remain so far away—deceivers and being deceived. The devil promised Jesus fame, fortune, even the hand of God to help Him (which of course he would not be able to produce—he is a liar), if He would but give him the worship upon which he feeds. Rooted in every temptation was taking the Bible out of context. Jesus rebutted every time with "It is written!"

The Amplified states Luke 4:13 this way:

> "And when the devil had ended every <the complete cycle of> temptation, he <temporarily> left Him <that is, stood off from Him> until another more opportune and favorable time."

The enemy is a plotter and planner. His intent is to bring us down, and everything that belongs to or is characteristic of Christ. Furthermore, he hates everything. His intent is to kill, steal, and destroy everything—even at that he will not be satisfied. He resembles a black hole, sucking everything he can into blackness void. He is cunning. He tempts, he watches, he waits—to what will they respond, which lure will they bite? To the individual and to the masses, he watches, he waits.

Why is it the very day we are going to lead worship—wham—we are bombarded with darkness, with distressing thoughts? We cannot really put our finger on exactly what we feel, we just feel bad, physically and emotionally. Is it just a natural reaction to the pressures of getting the song list together, planning the accompanying instruments, and organizing the stage? Maybe, but I doubt it. Spiritual rotten tomatoes are hurling, and we are the bulls-eye. Worship—a time set apart for God, and to bring people into a place of tenderized hearts and to hear God speak—the enemy is going to do what he can (within his tether) to stop, hinder, and bring chaos to God's plan. That is the enemy's plan; if he cannot stop us, he wants to bring chaos and shadows. He is persuasive and skilled at what he does, but nowhere near comparable to God. This time stop the enemy, instead of him stopping you. Rebuke him who is darkness personified. Begin to thank the Lord. Enter His gates with thanksgiving, taking thoughts captive; realign the focal point, Jesus Christ, to His rightful place.

By the grace of God never be outwitted by the enemy again.

Conclusion

* *

Struggles in the Prophetic

Struggles in the Prophetic began with personal stories relating to a couple of my own battles with the enemy. Even though I do not deal with condemnation as I used to, I remain on guard watching for the black cloud, the enemy's maneuvering, and tactics. We have all experienced victory in an area only to find we are again battling the very thing we thought we had victory over. The truth is, we did get victory, we did win the battle, we did not give in to the tempter, but now he's dexterously plotting and planning how to overtake us; is this an opportune time for him to take back the ground we conquered? We all have experienced victories, now we must learn to possess our land. Let us submit ourselves, then, to God. Resist the devil, and he will flee from us. (James 4:7)

Peter had a prophetic revelation but did not possess his land. Peter, in Acts 10, has a colossal prophetic revelation about the Gentiles acceptance into the Kingdom of God. The statement from God to Peter is, "Do not call anything impure that God has made clean." God spoke this to Peter three times! Although, the initial revelation was about food, God related it to Gentiles with his visit to Cornelius. "(Peter) said to them: 'You are well aware that it is against our law for a Jew to associate with a Gentile or visit him. But God has shown me that I should not call any man impure or unclean.'" This experience seems it would have transformed Peter's understanding forever, that the Gentiles are no different from the Jews in the Kingdom of God. Additionally, what God has accepted, Peter had better accept too.

Contrast Acts 10 with Galatians 2. When Peter was in Antioch, Paul confronted Peter to his face—because he was to blame. Peter would eat with the Gentiles only until the Jews showed up, then he would withdraw from them for fear of the Jews. Peter's hypocrisy spread to other Jews as well, even to Barnabas. Peter did not live out his life in view of what God had shown him with regard to the Gentiles and Cornelius. Peter, overtaken by the fear (mentioned in Galatians 2), lived in contradiction to the revelation he received in Acts 10.

Fear comes from an enemy, whether self-imposed by the flesh or demonic. Timothy may have fallen prey to fear, too. Paul told Timothy to stir up the gift, which was in him, because God had not given him a spirit of fear, but of power, love, and a sound mind. Peter and Timothy were both shrinking back due to fear. Both should have built upon the prophetic revelation given to them. They both, however, needed to be spurred on again (in both of these cases, by Paul), and reminded about the prophetic revelation given to each of them.

God speaks to us for a reason. If you have prophecies for your life, revisit them, and ask God for His intent in speaking them to you. When needed, stir up God's deposit within you.

Chapter 4

Proper Response to the Prophetic

PRAYER

Sick for Many Days

WORSHIP

Intercession

REPENTENCE

OBEDIENCE

RUNNING

SALVATIONS

Missions

Spiritual Enlightenment

Healing

DEatH (Acts 5)

Proclamation of the Message

Tears

FALLING FACE DOWN

Undone/Ruined

Change of Course

Strategies for Life

Boldness

Fainting

Remembering

...ARE JUST SOME OF THE PROPER RESPONSES TO THE PROPHETIC.

Introduction

• •

Proper Response to the Prophetic

FROM TIME TO TIME ALL OF US HAVE PROBABLY SAID, "That was such a powerful prophecy. God spoke so clearly about _____." However, 15 minutes later, none of us remembers the first thing about what He said. The Bible has many prophecies from beginning to end, all of them written down so the hearers would remember (and respond correctly) to them. The Bible frequently records people's responses along with the prophetic revelation; each prophecy requiring a different response, depending upon what God said, and what the hearers' were directed by the Holy Spirit to do. As we read the Bible, we see problems accrued when the people who heard the prophetic message did nothing in response to the prophetic revelation, or responded incorrectly. Numbers 14 is a recorded example of a wrong response to a word from God.

Wisdom records prophecies, carefully prays over them, and discusses the content to determine if the Holy Spirit indeed spoke. Then, once determined as authentically God, what is the proper response to His message? God speaks for a reason. When a church or individual responds correctly to a prophetic revelation, God blesses them in their obedience. How many difficulties would people have avoided had they first heard from the Holy Spirit, and then obeyed what He said?

Prophecy speaks to the past, present, and future. Through prophetic revelation God brings the past into context, "This *happened* because of this...," brings context to the present, "This is *happening* because of this...," and gives preparation guidance for the future, "This is *going to* happen, do this." Joshua 7 shows how the prophetic can bring light to current situations by revealing the past. Ai surprisingly defeated Israel. Joshua cried out to God, God told Joshua sin was the reason their enemies defeated them. Joshua prophesies to the people (Joshua 7:13), then God reveals to Joshua how to respond correctly. Joshua responds appropriately, Israel again goes against Ai, this time with complete victory.

Acts 27 recounts Paul's angelic visitation while on a ship as a prisoner. The angel gave Paul revelation about his future, and instruction for the men on the ship saying that the lives of the men would be safe if they stayed aboard the ship. There was a horrific storm. Paul was able to give the men courage during the voyage because of the angelic revelation. When some of the men started to sneak off the ship, Paul told them what the angel said. They stayed aboard, and all lives were saved. A wrong response to this prophetic revelation would have meant their death. s

This section is a study of a few proper responses to the prophetic.

Elijah

A. Read 1 Kings 17:1 and 18:41–46
   a. Identify the prophetic

   b. Identify intercession

   c. Identify faith

   d. Identify persistence

Daniel

A. Read Daniel 8:26–27
   What was Daniel's response to this vision?

B. Read Daniel 9:1–5
   a. Identify the prophetic

   b. Identify intercession

   c. Identify faith

Moses

Read Exodus 32:9–14
  a. Identify the prophetic

  b. Identify intercession

  c. Identify faith

Hezekiah

Read Isaiah 37:1–22a
  a. Identify the prophetic

  b. Identify intercession

  c. Identify faith

Read the following scriptures, and then write a brief summary describing how each person responded to the prophetic, whether they were the one initially hearing from God, or the recipient of the prophetic word spoken by another person.

a. Judges 7:13–15

b. John 1:47–49

c. John 4:16–30

d. Acts 13:2–4

e. 1 Timothy 1:18–19

f. Revelation 1

g. 2 Chronicles 15:8

Different revelations of the prophetic necessitate different responses. For example, the proper response to Jonah's prophecy to Nineveh was repentance for both Jonah and Nineveh. The proper response for Paul and Barnabas (Acts 13:2–4) was to have hands laid on them, and then be sent away. Sometimes the proper response is to say nothing except to God in prayer, especially if the anointing to prophesy is not present, or if the revelation does not give direction on what to do. Then, as we patiently wait on the Lord, and pray about the revelation, frequently, God will give further instruction.

Elijah heard the sound of rain prophetically, before the rain came physically. God spoke to Elijah that the time for rain, which he had prophesied three years earlier, had come. Elijah heard rain spiritually first (1 Kings 18:41), then went to Mount Carmel and prayed. He had his servant look seven times until he finally saw the cloud rising out of the sea. Elijah recognized the hand of God when it was still a small cloud on the horizon. He believed God, even when the rain was not yet recognizable as rain. He, then acted upon the prophetic revelation, saying to Ahab, "Prepare your chariot, and go down before the rain stops you."

The Lord spoke to Daniel in many different ways. He spoke to him through dreams, visions, angelic visitations, and through other prophets' writings. In Daniel 8, Daniel was watching a vision take place much like a movie. Daniel recounts, while experiencing the vision, angels speaking to him, lifting him up, God speaking to him and to the angels, watching himself in third person, and listening to angels talking to each other. Daniel 8 describes an extremely profound and expansive prophecy, spanning centuries of time. Kings and nations would rise and fall, Christ would be born, live and die before the fulfillment. God foretold the skeletal details beforehand, through, and to, Daniel. Daniel responds to the vision (Daniel 8:27) by exhaustion. He lay ill for several days, appalled by the vision—it was beyond understanding.

As Daniel read the Prophet Jeremiah, he realized that God had told Jeremiah 66 years earlier the captivity of Jerusalem would last 70 years. (Daniel 9:2) Since Jeremiah received this revelation from the Lord 66 years earlier, it meant there were four years until the fulfillment of the prophecy, and the end of captivity for Jerusalem. Because Daniel believed what God had spoken through Jeremiah, the prophet, he engaged with God according to the prophecy he read by prayer, confession, supplications, and fasting, with humility. Daniel did not just acknowledge the prophecy or talk about it—he believed it, therefore he sought God; his actions lined up with his beliefs. At the end of Daniels prayer and confession, he had another visitation from an angel—this time it was Gabriel. Gabriel revealed the Messianic 70-week prophecy to Daniel, such a great way to end a prayer time!

God spoke to Moses revealing His burning anger towards the rebellious and stiff-necked Hebrews in Exodus 32. God was seriously going to destroy them, and make Moses into a great nation. Moses instead interceded for the people, using God's own words and promises, while he sought the favor of the Lord on their behalf. Moses brought up Abraham, Isaac, and Israel and reflected upon the prophetic promises God had made to them. Moses reminded God of the Egyptians. What would they say about God if He destroyed His people? Moses knew God's heart, and knowing God's heart gave him confidence that he could approach the Lord this way. Moses also knew that God would relent from doing harm, as He did with Nineveh. He knew the story of Abraham pleading with God for Sodom and Gomorrah in Genesis 18:32, "Then he [Abraham] said, 'May the Lord not be angry, but let me speak just once more. What if only ten can be found there?' He [God] answered, 'For the sake of ten, I will not destroy it.'"

Since Moses knew God, he interceded for the people of God according to God's heart, God's own words, and the prophetic promises He had made to Abraham, Isaac, and Israel.

Initially, Hezekiah's faith manifests (in this account) when he sends men to Isaiah the prophet because of the threats of Sennacherib, king Assyria. Isaiah prophesies to Hezekiah that he is not to fear Sennacherib. Sennacherib would hear a rumor, return to his own land, and there he would be killed. Sennacherib sends word again to Hezekiah through a threatening letter. Hezekiah, however, lays out the letter before the Lord and prays. Isaiah 37:6 reveals God took it personally when the Assyrians mocked Him. Hezekiah brings this up before the Lord in Isaiah 37:17. As Hezekiah prays, he deflects the threats, which Sennacherib intended to produce fear in Hezekiah, back onto the Lord. Even though God had said He would take care of Sennacherib, God commends Hezekiah for continuing to pray in line with what God had spoken through Isaiah. Hezekiah believed what God spoke through Isaiah, and, *therefore* he prayed in agreement with God's word.

I have always thought this account of Gideon showed God's humor. A barley loaf representing Gideon, humorously, would not line up with any dream interpretation books. The prophetic came by way of a Midianite's dream, which Gideon just happened to overhear. (Once again, we see God speaking to and through a person who is not one of His own.) When Gideon heard it, it produced such a tremendous amount of faith in him that he worshipped, and then proclaimed victory to the others. Gideon's faith in what God said, through the prophetic dream, led to a supernatural victory.

Jesus spoke a prophetic revelation to Nathaniel in John 1:47–49. This prophetic revelation had such a dramatic affect on Nathaniel that he believed and declared Jesus was the Son of God, the King of Israel. 1 Corinthians 14 says Nathaniel's experience is exactly what would happen when an unbeliever encounters the prophetic, "But if an unbeliever or someone who does not understand comes in while everybody is prophesying, he will be convinced by all that he is a sinner and will be judged by all, and *the secrets of his heart will be laid bare.* So he will fall down and worship God, exclaiming, 'God is really among you!'" Jesus saw Nathaniel in such a way that when He told Nathaniel the revelation, Nathaniel knew it was from God. This opened Nathaniel's heart to believe and proclaim that Jesus was the Son of God. Now that is a prophetic revelation!

In the account from John 4:16–42, Jesus had a prophetic revelation leading a whole city to believe Him. Jesus spoke a word of knowledge to the Samaritan woman He met at the well. People of the city first came to hear Jesus because the Samaritan woman's testimony made them interested enough to come out to where Jesus was and listen to Him. They then believed in Him and said to the woman, "We no longer believe just because of what you said; now we have heard for ourselves, and we know that this man really is the Savior of the world." The prophetic revelation, spoken by Jesus to the woman at the well, opened the door to the city.

At some point in Timothy's life God had spoken to him through prophetic messages. These messages spoke to the destiny and calling upon Timothy's life ("so that by following them you may fight the good fight" [1 Timothy 1:18]). God's intent, through the prophecies, was to help Timothy stray on track, keep the faith, and protect his conscience. Some relate this to 2 Timothy 1:6 where Paul told Timothy to "fan into flame the gift of God," which was in him through the laying on of Paul's hands. It sounds plausible God revealed to Timothy, by way of these prophetic messages referred to in 1 Timothy 1:18-19, that trials, temptation, or attacks were coming his way; things which had shipwrecked others' faith, so that he could endure through them victoriously. Paul names both Hymenaeus and Alexander as those among the shipwrecked faith. In order to learn a lesson, Paul had handed them over to Satan.

The Revelation of Jesus Christ promises a blessing whoever reads or hears the words of its prophecy, and keeps the things written in it. In the *Book of Revelation*, Jesus prophesied to the churches in Asia, through letters written by the Apostle John. Jesus praised the churches, gave them encouragement, instruction, and warned them to repent where needed. Jesus spoke to each church in order to get a response from them. Throughout history (and still today) God is looking for a response from all who read *Revelation*. Initially, to arouse a hunger within people to read and hear the words of the prophecy, allowing the Holy Spirit to speak to them as He wills. Then also, to those who will be living on the earth during the fulfillment of the prophecies, to have faith and strength through to the end of this age. *The Revelation of Jesus Christ*, is filled with the glory, majesty and sovereignty of Jesus Christ—all of it prophetic. No matter what we face, Revelation 1:8 should inspire courage and faith within its readers, "I am the Alpha and the Omega," says the Lord God, "who is, and who was, and who is to come, the Almighty." John saw Jesus in a vision. When he saw Him, John's response was "he fell at His Feet as dead." Jesus tells John in the vision to, "Write, therefore, what you have seen, what is now and what will take place later." John's proper response was to write it down and send the revelation to the churches.

Topic for discussion: Joseph: Genesis 37:3–20

During our small group studies on Joseph, we discussed differing opinions about Joseph's intent in revealing the dreams to his family, since his brothers already hated him and his father favored him.

Do you think Joseph responded correctly to his prophetic dream by telling his brothers and father what God showed him?

Discuss faith in view of God speaking a prophetic revelation, and then the exact opposite happening (Joseph was looking up at his brothers from the bottom of a pit, instead of them looking up at him). What would God's purpose be in revealing the revelation knowing Joseph would soon be at the bottom of the pit?

Conclusion

• •

Proper Response to the Prophetic

To conclude Proper Response to the Prophetic, look at three scriptures from Revelation:

- "I was in the Spirit on the Lord's day, and I heard behind me a loud voice like the sound of a trumpet, saying, 'Write in a book what you see, and send it to the seven churches: to Ephesus and to Smyrna and to Pergamum and to Thyatira and to Sardis and to Philadelphia and to Laodicea.'" (Revelation 1: 10–11, NAS)

- "Write the things which you have seen, and the things which are, and the things which will take place after this." (Revelation 1:19, NAS)

Packed into these three scriptures is a wealth of instruction and revelation. First of all, John is "in the Spirit." When God reveals Kingdom matters to us while we are "in the Spirit" or "under the anointing of the Holy Spirit," what He reveals makes sense to us, whereas outside the anointing, doubtless they would seem ridiculous to our natural mindset. If we do not record what God revealed while we are "in the Spirit," the revelation can easily be lost, forever forgotten, or reasoned away.

> THAT IS THE PROPHETIC— IN THE SPIRIT SEEING AND HEARING THINGS PAST, PRESENT, AND OR FUTURE— THINGS, WHICH BRING GLORY TO GOD AND HELP TO PEOPLE.

In *The Revelation*, Jesus describes Himself as, The Eternal One, The Beginning and The End, The First and The Last. Jesus tells John to write down what he sees, and then send it to the seven churches: things that you have seen (past), the things that are (present), and the things that will take place after these things (future). That is the prophetic—in the Spirit seeing and hearing things past, present, and or future—things, which bring glory to God and help to people.

All the prophecies in the Bible have one response in common, someone wrote them down. It seems simple, but it is true. Someone took the time to record for all what God said. Imagine the Bible without the scribes. Imagine the prophets without the pen. So much would be lost and forgotten forever, apart from direct revelation through the Holy Spirit.

When we do not record what the Holy Spirit says, it is easy to forget what He said, either in part or altogether. Pay attention to the conditions God spells out as He speaks. Many claim the promises without walking through the conditions. Our response most often determines whether we inherit the promises. Record what He says. Pray about the details. Agree with His words, and as the years go by you will be glad you did.

Chapter 5

....

Prophetic Gifts and the Local Church

But everything should be done in a fitting and orderly way.
1 Corinthians 14:40

For God is not a God of disorder but of peace.
As in all the congregations of the saints...
1 Corinthians 14:33

What then shall we say, brothers? When you come together, everyone has a hymn, or a word of instruction, a revelation, a tongue or an interpretation. All of these must be done for the strengthening of the church.
1 Corinthians 14:26

Obey your leaders and submit to their authority. They keep watch over you as men who must give an account. Obey them so that their work will be a joy, not a burden, for that would be of no advantage to you.
Hebrews 13:17

In essentials, unity; in non-essentials, liberty; in all things, charity.
Augustine

Introduction

◆ ◆

Prophetic Gifts and the Local Church

IN ESSENTIALS, UNITY; IN NON-ESSENTIALS, LIBERTY; IN ALL THINGS, CHARITY. (AUGUSTINE) How spiritual gifts ought to operate within the local church is only vaguely described in the Bible, and because of this, there is large variation from church to church. Clearly emphasized, however, is that gifts are to manifest. This chapter looks at five very different churches showing the variations, in style and leading of the Holy Spirit within each local church. The Bible states the gifts are to operate in an orderly and yielding way, judged and evaluated by the hearers, and are to bring encouragement, comfort, and exhortation to the people, and sometimes warning and direction, as well as foretelling.

Leaders should seek the Lord concerning the operation of spiritual gifts in the church they shepherd. Guidelines, not laws, should be established and openly presented to the people, so that everyone will know what to do when they have a revelation from the Lord. God places it solely upon the leaders of each church to set these guidelines, dependent on how the Holy Spirit is directing the flow of spiritual gifts in the church they shepherd. A word of caution: since the Bible is vague on the operation of spiritual gifts within local assemblies, it is necessary for leaders to allow flexibility for the leading of the Holy Spirit to manifest His gifts outside the established guidelines and personal comfort zones. Throughout the Bible, God often did the unexpected. We must remain open to Him.

When leaders do not establish and present clearly defined guidelines, frequently confusion and disorder replace them. Spiritual gifts, though different between the Old and New Testaments, are prominent in the Bible beginning to end, and they should be a regular part of church life. When spiritual gifts are not taught and practiced, it is much like a church leader who would not allow teaching, or the practice of water baptisms, since water baptisms get people and the church floor wet, and wet people do not belong in church.

"Where there are no oxen, the manger is empty, but from the strength of an ox comes an abundant harvest." (Proverbs 14:4) The exercise of spiritual gifts within a local church is much like this scripture. Accompanying spiritual gifts will be excess and mistakes but the benefits far outweigh the cost of feeding the ox or cleaning his messes.

Following are a few testimonies where a revelation from the Holy Spirit gave guidance and a tactical plan for a local church.

We were a part of a church of about 375 people. Half of the congregation was single people, college-aged, mostly students, and the other half were families. The church spent a tremendous amount of resources on the college-aged group during the winter months when school was in session. However, during the summer, since most of them were gone, the church somewhat coasted along until the next school year began. During a time of corporate prayer, the Lord revealed a movie in my spirit of a large deciduous tree. As the movie played, the tree went through different lifecycle stages with each season. In spring, the tree was fertilized producing new growth. Shoots, buds, and leaves appeared. As the lifecycle progressed, the buds turned to flowers. The flowers then turned to fruit, and when the maturing fruit ripened, it was harvested providing nourishment for others. In autumn, the leaves turned color, and the wind blew the leaves and seeds off the tree, to their predetermined places set by the Lord. Then the cycle began again. The Lord said our church was that tree and we, too, had seasons, each season with a different purpose and focus. In this revelation, the Lord gave His strategy for our church during the summer months when the college students were gone. We were to strengthen the trunk and the over-all health of the tree by fertilizing heavily the year-rounders with targeted teaching and focus during the summer; turning the attention of nearly all resources towards this goal, to make us stronger and healthier as a whole.

A large church that I am friends with does a week of fasting every January. Many corporate prayer meetings engage daily during this week as the church looks to the Lord for fresh direction, and for strategy to win the city for Jesus Christ. One year the Lord spoke clearly about starting house churches (small groups, cell groups, etc.). The leaders took a full year to prepare the church adequately. During the year, they identified and trained house church leaders, and when the time came, a year later, the response was overwhelming. A majority of the church participated, and the church flourished. They are wise leaders.

This example is of leaders who did not follow the Lord's voice and the results. A leader from our fellowship of churches came to our church to preach. The night before he was to preach, he had a dream. In the dream, the Lord said He would speak prophetically about water flowing though our church, and the dream coupled with the prophecies, was to confirm that the Holy Spirit was going to move mightily during the meeting. God spoke prophetically about water flowing through our church in two prophecies. This gave the guest pastor great confidence to move out in what the Lord had told him. He would preach a little, then prophesy, then preach some more. The visiting pastor would give a specific personal prophecy (which we all knew was accurate because we were a tightly knit group of people), then he would look at the leaders and prophesy, "Do not go back to business as usual..." Repeatedly this happened. "Do not go back to business as usual; I am visiting the youth..." Then he would preach, then prophesy, and on and on for 6 hours! Our leaders rejected the word of the Lord, going back to business as usual. Church attendance declined from 400 to 100 over a couple years. Many believe the church lost its call to carry the torch in our city. God has strategies, which have not entered our minds. We must listen to Him.

Administration and Guidelines

Following are guidelines from a local church. They are included only as an example.

1. Designate a prophetic overseer in the church who must be:
   - someone who is seasoned in revelatory gifts
   - able to discern the corporate anointing
   - able to discern what God wants to accomplish during the service
   - responsible to evaluate prophetic words before they are spoken publicly
   - able to nurture and help people who are immature in their gifts
   - able to teach on the revelatory gifts
   - submitted to leadership, able to work within the framework and vision of the church

2. Have a prophetic group that operates much like a small group/home group within the local church. Having a prophetic group will provide a platform for an increase in the anointing upon the prophetic in the church by:
   - providing directed prayer for the prophetic
   - prayer over the prophetic words spoken
   - praying for each other
   - building up the inexperienced
   - increasing unity among the group (Psalms 133)
   - mutual guidelines
   - directed teaching
   - shared vision
   - mutual encouragement

3. A prophetic group will increase accountability in the prophetic by:
   - requiring a leader's referral
   - giving and receiving feedback from others
   - providing safe boundaries within the framework of a small group to exercise spiritual gifts
   - providing guidelines to help the inexperienced

4. General guidelines for the prophetic:
   Personal Prophecies:
   (Guidelines for those who prophesy personal prophecies to individuals)
   - directive prophecy should have a witness
   - personal prophecies should have a witness and it's a good idea to take notes
   - no personal words during the worship service or preaching
   - those who prophesy must regularly attend a small group unless exempt by the elders
   Public Prophecies:
   (Guidelines for those who prophesy publicly to the local church)
   - must submit word to prophetic overseer before prophesying
   - speak the word not your words about the word
   - must regularly attend a small group unless exempt by the elders
   - must be recommended by a small group leader to the elders
   - must speak strengthening, encouragement and comfort to the hearers

Prophetic Gifts in the Local Church

Example churches below are churches, George, and I have had the privilege to be a part of or to know the leaders. As you can see from these examples, churches can have vastly differing styles and protocol, but it is still the same Holy Spirit at work in each church. (1 Corinthians 12)

Church 1 The church referred to in "Administration and Guidelines" is similar to another church I know. Both churches had point people who screened corporate revelations before people prophesied. The screener had to be a uniquely gifted individual. Their position had the ability to injure people and stunt another's spiritual growth, if they lacked wisdom or grace in handling delicate situations and people; therefore, their spiritual maturity was essential. Along with freedom from prejudgments and prejudices, the screener had to be someone who would not manipulate people or the anointing. The screener would:

1. Ensure the revelation was biblical
2. Ensure the message was clear and formulated
3. Help the person get at the heart of what the Lord revealed, when needed
4. Prevent embarrassment and preserve dignity when the "revelation" was not the Lord
5. Build confidence in the person by affirmation of what was heard from the Lord
6. Provide an orderly avenue for gifts—so people would know who to talk to and when
7. Ensure another leader, lost in worship, was not interrupted

This church also had a prophetic group, which met weekly. As a group, we would discuss and pray about the prophetic revelations the Lord had spoken during the weekly corporate meetings, and then write a summary for the weekly bulletin's *Prophetic Corner*. Together, as a small group, we studied *Soaring in the Prophetic*, and practiced exercising spiritual gifts. Throughout each week, we would pray, specifically, for a member of the group. The following meeting they would get the "Hot Seat." We would pray for them, and practice exercising spiritual gifts as we prayed. It was great fun and very rewarding. Graduation night (the last night of the small group), a pastoral leader with a strong prophetic gift would join us, releasing each graduate to be used in revelatory gifts corporately.

Both of these churches had an abundance of spiritual gifts operating in each service. Many times the prophetic words spoken before the preaching would be nearly identical to the pastor's message, which was radically encouraging. The service would start with worship, and then flow into a time for spiritual gifts, followed by the preaching. After the preaching, usually words of knowledge would manifest, followed by prayer from designated people for those who responded. From time to time, other revelatory gifts would follow the service as well.

When someone had a directional word from the Lord, which affected the congregation at large, guidelines required they first discuss it with one of the lead pastors, apart from the Sunday service. This would give the leader opportunity to pray over and talk to other leaders about it first, to find the Lord's intended response. Sometimes he would share it with the congregation, sometimes he implemented what the Lord said without telling the congregation where the idea originated, sometimes he had the person share the revelation, and other times nothing except prayer (as far as I know) occurred.

Church 2   I appreciate the leadership of this church. Their wisdom and love for the people they shepherded is unmistakable. Many different levels of maturity and understanding of spiritual gifts exist among the congregation, since it is a large church. Weekly prayer meetings began at the church's inception and continue today. Most of the spiritual gifts manifest within these prayer meetings (and within the small groups), and since it is within the prayer meetings, the revelations, if they are from the Lord, receive immediate prayer when they are shared. Then, during the Sunday church service, the pastor reiterates the main messages or themes, which the Holy Spirit spoke through His gifts during the prayer meeting. This is so the whole church can hear the Holy Spirit's message. When the pastor receives a prophetic revelation privately from someone, which he believes is for the church at large, he will share the prophecy publicly with the congregation. In the years we were part of this assembly, I only saw someone go to the microphone two times with a word from the Lord during the corporate Sunday meeting; however, spiritual gifts flourish within this church.

Church 3   Another church I am friends with varies vastly with the church above in the flow if their corporate meetings. The leader is a man of the Spirit and truly loves the presence of God, and the supernatural. He is a trailblazer in the region; he boldly goes where no man has gone before. Spiritual gifts flow in this church on a regular basis. Leadership usually manifests the revelatory gifts of the Spirit corporately, during the church service. If an open microphone existed, church may go on for hours since a tremendous number of people exist within the church that could (and would) manifest spiritual gifts. When another (who is not in leadership), has a revelation, it is not easy to know what to do or who to ask for permission to speak corporately what the Lord has revealed. Personal prophecies and ministry to one another is continually happening, especially during worship, fellowship time, and after the service. From time to time guest speakers will come and hold meetings, many centered on the revelatory gifts. This keeps the corporate church open to the gifts of the Spirit, and to the supernatural. Spirit-led evangelism and healing flourish in this church, as well.

Church 4   I smile as I think of this leader because he is truly a man of God. Seeing him in many different situations and trials, he remains strong in each, and though beaten and bruised, he forges ahead. This leader had seasons (a few weeks at a time) for targeted teaching on spiritual gifts. In these meetings, opportunities for spiritual gifts to manifest existed. People who had teaching gifts, coupled with people gifted in the prophetic, taught these classes in order to gain experience. The pastor noted who the accurate prophetic people were and would ask them to join him in prophetic evangelism. We had great fun, and with much fruit!

During the Sunday services, prophetic words manifested from time to time, and there was always freedom to do so. However, most of the prophetic occurred during evangelism and the targeted prophetic meetings.

This pastor also interfaced with the local university, which offered a one-credit class on Christianity. Our pastor's goal was two-fold: to *teach* about Christianity, and to make sure the students *experienced* Christianity. During this class, the university students would come to our church for their class period. We would pray for the students and prophesy to them; most often, they experienced the manifestation of the Kingdom of God in one way or another. One weekend a term, the students would come to our church for numerous meetings. The weekend began with a shared dinner between the church community and the students on Friday night. After dinner, there was teaching and demonstration of the revelatory gifts. Saturday, the students were back at our church for more meetings with teaching and more revelatory gifts. Ending the weekend, the students would join our church service on Sunday and again experience God. It was great fun, and many people encountered the reality of Jesus Christ for the first time during these classes.

Church 5   Spiritual gifts operated in Church 5 during the Wednesday night midweek service, which the church coined as Family Night. Church 5 was a large church, and therefore like Church 2 above, they had many diverse backgrounds, levels of maturity, and varying knowledge of spiritual gifts. In order to keep the flow of spiritual gifts within the church, the pastor and leaders decided to keep the midweek Family Nights open to the revelatory gifts. Doing this also kept Sundays as a time to focus on visitors or less "churched" people." Family Night consisted mainly of core people who had more experience with and knowledge of spiritual gifts. In midweek services, operation of spiritual gifts would flow much like Church 1.

Words of Knowledge

I have had the opportunity to observe how several churches administer words of knowledge. As stated, biblical directives for administration of revelatory gifts within corporate gatherings is vague, and consequently for leaders to decide, as led by the Holy Spirit. However, words of knowledge are usually, as a guideline, best spoken at the end of meetings, because they have the unique ability to direct the course of the entire church meeting, if spoken earlier. This is another reason it is important to have someone overseeing the prophetic ministry who is mature enough to screen revelations appropriately. Additionally, keeping words of knowledge for the end of the service provides an opportunity for those who respond to receive immediate prayer without disrupting the overall flow of the church service.

In churches I either have been a part of or have visited, it was common to see a point person with a word of knowledge gift. One church had individuals who received words of knowledge from the Lord communicate them to the point person. The point person, then in turn, read them aloud, one by one, waiting for a response after each. In another church, the point person displayed the words of knowledge on overhead projection. People then responded after reading the display. I have also seen words of knowledge read all together, and then people respond more as a group. Other churches had an open microphone at the end of the service. Individuals would themselves say what God has spoken to them, whether a word of knowledge, or other revelatory gifts.

How each church handles words of knowledge during their church meetings varies with each church. We should flow with our leaders' administration of spiritual gifts. The concern is not *how* spiritual gifts flow, but rather that spiritual gifts *are* free to flow somewhere in the life of our church.

End of Service Prayer

Many churches have prayer at the end of the service. Prayer teams or other leaders usually stand at the front of the room prepared to pray with and for those who want to receive Jesus Christ, for general needs, and those who respond to a revelation (as a word of knowledge). This not only allows opportunity for those with prayer needs to receive prayer, but there is an added benefit: It also helps people know who the leaders are. Additionally, in an unusual way, it makes people feel more at ease and "at home." People can decide in advance which person they feel comfortable going to for prayer. Furthermore, they will not find an empty spot when they arrive. We forget how intimidating it can be for people to respond to an empty alter. Having someone greet us as we respond is much more inviting and welcoming.

Conclusion

• •

Prophetic Gifts and the Local Church

Administration of spiritual gifts varies in each church community. Our focus and energy spent on what matters to God, not our own opinions and wants, leads to a healthy flow of spiritual gifts and community. God warns, "Do not put out the Spirit's fire; do not treat prophecies with contempt. Test everything. Hold on to the good." (1 Thessalonians 5:19-21) The whole community of believers has a responsibility to flow with the Holy Spirit, and not to put out our hand to steady Him as Uzzah did at the threshing floor of Kidon. (1 Chronicles 13:9) Many churches have walked away from their call as they have put out their hand to steady the ark, when the ark was supposed to steady them. "Test everything. Hold on to the good" is the remedy for dealing with well meaning people who miss the mark when they manifest the revelatory gifts and not, "Let us avoid mistakes by never allowing revelatory gifts."

God sometimes gives extremely precise details on how He wants to build and other times He does not. For example, God gave Moses precise instruction for building the tabernacle and all its furnishings. (Exodus 25:9, 25:40) Consequently, the artistic work for the lampstand (Exodus 25) had meticulous details, and yet, God left some room for the artist's own inspiration. Interestingly, Jesus interprets the seven golden lampstands, which John saw in Revelation 1, as the seven churches (Revelation 1:20). Some details in His church are to be meticulously precise and other details flow with the personality of the leaders, and the community of believers represented. However, a lampstand has the purpose of providing a place for fire—and the *Fire* was never to go out. This *Fire* is the Holy Spirit. (Revelation 4:5) People of God—do not put out the Spirit's fire. As we build, one thing is certain, we must build in such a way that our church is a habitation for Fire—His Fire. As His Fire burns, the natural reaction is for His gifts to manifest. Churches that do not allow for the manifestation of spiritual gifts are quenching the Spirit's fire; this environment quickly becomes problematic for Spirit-filled Christians, and they will eventually find another church.

Administration for the Holy Spirit's gifts in the New Testament is much like the lampstand—some precise details, and some broad principles. We should flow with our leaders and fellow Christians. They will miss the mark from time to time, and so will we. If we have an idea, let us share it with our leaders. If they like it, great, if they do not, leave it alone. How spiritual gifts are to flow in churches is not a formula, rather it necessitates an ability to hear God for His plan for each church. God, otherwise, would have given clear and precise instructions in His word, as He did other things. Nevertheless, if we are disgruntled, murmur, and complain, causing division and pain to our leaders, and fellow believers, God will not take it lightly. Let us follow the way of love instead. Work with the church and not against her. When we cannot flow within our community of believers, then it is time to find a place where we can. Not all churches are for everyone, but The Church is.

"Above all, love each other deeply, because love covers over a multitude of sins." (1 Peter 4:8)

Chapter 6

Gifts of the Spirit

Each one should use whatever gift he has
Received to serve others, faithfully administering
God's grace in its various forms.

1 Peter 4:10

Instead, speaking the truth in love, we will in all things grow up into him who is the head,
that is, Christ. From him the whole body, joined and held together by every supporting
ligament, grows and builds itself up in love, as each part does its work.

Ephesians 4:15–16

Introduction

❖ ❖

Gifts of the Spirit

CHAPTER 5 DISCUSSED HANDLING OF THE PROPHETIC gifts in the local church, while chapter 6 defines and gives examples of the gifts listed in the New Testament. Spiritual gifts should manifest anywhere there are Christians.

Ephesians 4:11-16 discusses the five governmental gifts—the 5-fold, given by Jesus. They are apostle, prophet, evangelist, pastor, and teacher. All five of these gifts are necessary for the building up of the body of Christ to maturity. However, most churches do not have all five equipping the saints within their local church. In the early church, some 5-fold leaders would travel throughout the churches in order to build the body of Christ. Ephesians 4 is clear that all five of these gifts are important, "...to prepare God's people for works of service, so that the body of Christ may be built up, Then we will no longer be infants, tossed back and forth by the waves, and blown here and there by every wind of teaching and by the cunning and craftiness of men in their deceitful scheming." (Ephesians 4:14) These five governmental gifts, operating as God intended, are rare in most church families today. Additionally, finding cities where the churches work together, offering each other services and support, are even rarer. However, I have seen it on a small scale in Oregon.

Along with the five governmental gifts, God, also gives other gifts of the Spirit to His people for the purpose of building up and edifying His church, and for ministry to the lost. Most accounts of spiritual gifts recorded in the Bible were in the market place. In scripture, there are three lists of general spiritual gifts; Romans 12, one list and two lists are in 1 Corinthians 12. A few other named gifts are scattered throughout the New Testament. Some people believe these lists are exhaustive while others do not. New Testament spiritual gifts, listed alphabetically are:

1. Administrations
2. Celibacy
3. Discerning of spirits
4. Exhortation
5. Faith
6. Gifts of Healings
7. Giving
8. Helps
9. Hospitality
10. Interpretation of Tongues
11. Leadership
12. *Martyrdom
13. Mercy
14. Miracles
15. Missionary
16. Prophecy
17. Service
18. Variety of Tongues
19. *Voluntary Poverty
20. Word of Knowledge
21. Word of Wisdom

*Martyrdom and voluntary poverty exist on some lists, but I believe they are expressions of gifts such as faith or missionary. (Deuteronomy 28 describes non-voluntary poverty as a curse.) They are, therefore, not included in the following definitions of spiritual gifts.

Definitions

• •

Gifts of the Spirit

Five Governmental Gifts (Ephesians 4:11)

Ephesians 4:11 lists five gifts that are apostle, prophet, evangelist, pastor, and teacher. These five are unique governmental gifts, given to people who then *become* the gift to the church. Their job is to governmentally build up and equip the church for works of ministry, *so that* the church will mature. Notice the wording: "And He [Jesus] gave some as apostles, and some as prophets, and some as evangelists, and some as pastors and teachers, for the equipping of the saints for the work of service, to the building up of the body of Christ…" (NAS) Therefore, these five governmental gifts stand alone in contrast to the non-governmental gifts listed later.

All Christians should have a vital and deep prayer-life, I have, therefore, not included prayer as a unique attribute to any of the characteristics when describing spiritual gifts.

 An apostle has a God-given special governmental endowment and calling to serve, strengthen, and build up the body of Christ by launching and leading new ministry ventures, which advance God's purpose and expand His Kingdom within a specific realm of influence. The original Greek meaning of the word is "sent one with orders" (literally, one sent with authority or as an ambassador). An apostle's calling in the Kingdom of God is much like an architect in a building project. The apostle may or may not be the lead governmental authority in a local church. People with this gift:

- Love the church
- Are sound in their approach to biblical doctrine
- Work as a team with others
- Are visionaries and see the "big picture"
- Have a unique calling to start new endeavors as directed by God, most often churches
- Willingly work hard to see churches mature and reach their full potential for God
- Often are called to oversee multiple churches or ministries
- Often have their sights on and travel to the nations
- Are known to welcome risky new challenges, as directed by the Holy Spirit
- Are known to operate in the supernatural
- Encounter many hardships

Prophet — New Testament prophets are different from Old Testament prophets. The New Testament prophet did not exist until Jesus ascended on high, thus making the Old Testament model obsolete (Ephesians 4:8-11, Luke 16:16). One of the root words for prophet is "to make known one's thoughts, to declare; therefore, the prophet makes known and declares the thoughts of God. The New Testament prophet has a God-given special governmental endowment and calling to serve, strengthen, and stir up the body of Christ, to hear God by teaching, demonstration of prophecy, in both forth telling and foretelling, and mentoring others to hear God. Since a prophet carries governmental authority, the prophet will also bring correction and warning when led by the Holy Spirit to do so. The prophet may or may not be the lead governmental authority in a local church. People with this gift:

- Love the church
- Are sound in their approach to biblical doctrine
- Are recognized by the church to have a high level prophetic ministry
- Have God-given spiritual vision for the church
- Are able to teach and equip others in the prophetic gifts
- Work as a team with others
- Many have spiritual experiences such as, audible voices, angelic visitations, visions, etc.
- Will passionately desire others to hear God's voice and know God's heart

Evangelist — An Evangelist has a God-given special governmental endowment and calling to serve, strengthen, and stir up the body of Christ toward evangelism. The Evangelist has a unique endowment to share the love of Christ in such a way that it draws people to respond to God, and thereby, receive God's gift of eternal life through Jesus Christ. The evangelist may or may not be the lead governmental authority in a local church. People with this gift:

- Love the church
- Are sound in their approach to biblical doctrine
- Are generally extroverts
- Work as a team with others
- Stir up the body of Christ to focus on the lost
- Identify with Jesus' heart that He came to seek and save that which is lost
- Equip the church how to share a coherent salvation message
- Can identify the needs of the city as Paul did in Athens (Acts 17) and Ephesus (Acts 19)
- Carry the heart of Jesus for the lost
- Evangelism comes naturally to them
- Must guard against feeling frustrated with others' focuses

Pastor — A pastor has a God-given special governmental endowment and calling to serve, strengthen, and build up the body of Christ as a shepherd. A pastor tends, nurtures, guards, guides, protects, and feeds God's sheep under his care (Acts 20:28, the definition of "poimaino," the Greek word translated as "shepherd"). According to the Greek Lexicon, "The tasks of a Near Eastern shepherd were: 1. to watch for enemies trying to attack the sheep, 2. to defend the sheep from attackers, 3. to heal the wounded and sick sheep, 4. to find and save lost or trapped sheep, 5. to love them, sharing their lives and so earning their trust." Shepherds with sheep are descriptive of New Testament pastors and their heart for the church and people in general. The pastor may or may not be the lead governmental authority in a local church. People with this gift:

- Love the church
- Love to be around people (i.e. to hang out with the sheep)
- Are sound in their approach to biblical doctrine
- Have a heart which yearns for people
- Have a heart which yearns for the community
- Desires people to walk in their calling and gifts
- Long to equip those around them with what is needed to become mature believers
- Watch over the church as a shepherd watches over sheep
- Are diligent to know the state of the flock
- Love to study and teach sound biblical doctrine with the purpose of feeding the sheep
- Are a team leaders
- Work with others to accomplish Holy Spirit given vision

A teacher has a God-given special governmental endowment and calling to serve, strengthen, and stir up the body of Christ towards the study of the scriptures and sound biblical doctrine. The teacher has a unique ability to share their love for the scriptures in such a way that it spurs and inspires biblical knowledge and education. The teacher has the ability to make difficult passages understandable. The teacher may or may not be the lead governmental authority in a local church. People with this gift:

- Love the church
- Are sound in their approach to biblical doctrine
- Desire and are able to equip the church by teaching sound biblical doctrine
- Desire to equip the church on how to study the Bible using sound exegesis principles
- Work as a team with others
- Are given to hours in the study of Scriptures, and love to do so
- Are capable teachers and enjoy making the Bible clear, relevant, and understandable
- Have passion for biblical truth
- Realize their dependence upon the Holy Spirit for understanding the scriptures

◆ ◆

Nongovernmental Spiritual Gifts

Non-governmental gifts of the Spirit are the God-given special endowments, given through the Holy Spirit, to share God's love, strengthen the body of Christ, and reach the lost. Gifts of the Spirit are always others-focused. The nongovernmental gifts of the Spirit are alphabetically ordered.

Administration

Gifts of of administration are the God-given special endowment to serve, strengthen, and build up the body of Christ and others, through governing, ruling, steering affairs, and providing operational guidance for the church or anywhere this gift is needed. 1 Corinthians 12:28 is the only place in scripture where this word "to govern" is found. It literally means, "guiding the helm of affairs," and therefore, coincides with the office of an elder or bishop, who is to rule and guide the affairs of the church, according to 1 Timothy. People with this gift:

- Have superb organizational skills
- Have superb business sense
- Can work well with others and under pressure
- Are visionary in operational tasks
- See needs others are unaware of
- Must be able to teach
- Must govern his own family well
- Must be hospitable
- Must be mature Christians
- Love the church

Celibacy

The gift of celibacy is the God-given special endowment to serve, strengthen, and build up the body of Christ and others by living an unmarried life in order to give undivided devotion to God. People with this gift not only live a single lifestyle; rather they live unmarried in order to devote themselves undividedly to God, and His work. The Apostle Paul, in 1 Corinthians 7, discusses this gift in detail. The Apostle Paul is an example of this gift in action. People with this gift:

- Choose not to marry either for lack of desire or as a sacrifice
- Frequently spend much time in studying the Bible
- Use their resources to further the Kingdom of God
- Use their resources to build the body of Christ
- Are often misunderstood by the church at large

| Discernment | Discernment is the God-given special endowment to serve, strengthen, and build up the body of Christ and others by having the ability to distinguish whether something is of the Holy Spirit, the human spirit, a |

demon, or an angel. An example of Paul operating in this gift is Acts 16:16–18. People with this gift can range from discerning an annoyance, sensing a change in the immediate atmosphere, a discomfort in their spirit, to seeing an open manifestation of a spirit. People with this gift must guard themselves not to become critical and judgmental, but instead, are to love people and the church desiring to build her up. People with this gift:

- If not taught about their gift, they may wonder if they are crazy because they sense, hear and/or see aspects of the spiritual world
- May hear other people's thoughts as the Holy Spirit reveals them
- Will suddenly sense a need to leave a situation or place
- May identify the source of a sickness, need, or trial
- May discern the spirit behind a message or speaker
- May see spirits whether angelic or demonic

| Exhortation/ Encouragement | Exhortation, also translated as encouragement, is the God-given special endowment to serve, strengthen, and build up the body of Christ and others by giving |

Holy Spirit inspired timely exhortations and encouragements, which spur on and or comfort those who hear. The Greek word is "paraklesis." Paraklesis has a broad definition ranging from an admonition, to comfort, to a persuasive discourse, or a strong urging. The heart of this word is to "come along side, to aid." Therefore, the gift will manifest in order to comfort and spur on the church and others, towards love and good works, both towards God and each other, in a wide-ranging approach. An example of Jesus operating in this gift is Mark 5:35–36; and Paul, in Acts 27. People who have this gift should be careful to speak as directed by the Holy Spirit, and not from their own soulish wisdom. People with this gift:

- Often desire to counsel people
- Are motivated to spur people on to believe God and His Word
- Are sometimes resisted when people feel the "spur"
- Desire to help people reach their full potential
- Are positive "you can do it" kind of people while under the anointing of the Holy Spirit, but can easily become "drivers" if they stray into carnality.
- Often are very direct because of their confidence in God
- Generally have a strong foundation in Bible knowledge

| Faith | The gift of faith is the God-given special endowment to serve, strengthen, and build up the body of Christ and others through extraordinary faith, given by the Holy Spirit, at specific times and in special circumstances. This gift differs |

from general faith, which Romans 12:3 states, "God has given to each one a measure of faith." Matthew 8:5–13 is an example of this gift. The gift of faith, which is often preceded by a word from the Lord, is so your faith does not rest in the wisdom of man but in the power of God. (1 Corinthians 2:5) People with this gift:

- Have extraordinary ability to believe what God has said
- Have great confidence even when circumstances look bleak
- Are often in leadership positions
- Are sometimes criticized for being over confident
- Often walk in the miraculous

Giving The gift of giving is the God-given special endowment to serve, strengthen, and build up the body of Christ and others by giving with singleness of heart in order to supply the needs of others. Wealth is not a prerequisite to having this gift. 1 Timothy 6:17–19 gives instruction to those who are rich in this world to be generous and giving; Philippians 4 describes a church with the gift of giving. People with this gift:

- Have a heart to minister to people materially
- Often operate in the word of knowledge
- See money and other material wealth as a vehicle for good
- Often organize others in order to meet needs
- Are often visionary

Healing Gifts of healing are God-given special endowments to serve, strengthen, and build up the body of Christ and others by healing those whom need healing whether, body, soul, or spirit. Gifts of healing often precede words of knowledge. The laying on of hands is often the means the Holy Spirit uses to heal, and sometimes with anointing oil. John 5 is an example of Jesus healing body, soul, and spirit to the man with infirmity at the Pool Bethesda. People with this gift:

- Often feel sensation in their own body corresponding to the need of healing in another
- Often operate in the word of knowledge, mercy, faith and compassion
- Usually are part of a prayer team
- Have a heart for shepherding and binding up the broken hearted
- Often skilled in counseling
- Should have strong Bible knowledge
- Often also have discerning of spirits

Helps The gift of helps is the God-given special endowment to serve, strengthen, and build up the body of Christ and others by supplying a service where there is lack, whether a natural or a spiritual lack. This gift manifests in the true nature of its title "helps" in the assistance of leaders, church meetings, gathering and distribution of alms, visiting those in prison, the hospital or at home, or *any place* where help is needed. The deacons in Acts 6 are an example of the gift of helps in action. The word "antilepsis," found only one time in the Bible, is translated as "helps." 1 Corinthians 12:28. People with this gift:

- See needs others do not
- Find joy in serving others
- Have a skill set in areas of use to others
- Are content to serve behind the scenes
- Identify with the Holy Spirit's nature of being a Helper (Romans 16:2, Hebrews 13:6)

Hospitality

The gift of hospitality is the God-given special endowment to serve, strengthen, and build up the body of Christ and others by ensuring others feel welcome, both inside and outside of the church. This is a unique Holy Spirit powered gift of hospitality and is not the same as general hospitality, which all Christians (especially overseers) are to be hospitable. Paul's letters frequently open with a hospitable greeting. Luke 10 gives account of Martha opening her home to Jesus, and Colossians 4:15 explains that Nympha had church in her house; both are examples of the hospitality gift. People with this gift:

- Are gifted with the ability to make others feel welcome
- Often open their houses to friends and strangers
- Use their resources for others
- Are often known as gatherers
- Are best suited if they have organizational skills
- Have a heart for the lonely and stranger

Interpretation of Tongues

Interpretation of Tongues is the God-given special endowment to serve, strengthen, and build up the body of Christ and others by understanding God's prophetic message spoken in tongues. A gift of tongues always precedes this gift. The interpretation of a tongue manifests either by revelation from the Holy Spirit or by naturally knowing the language spoken in the tongue. The purpose of this gift, when coupled with the gift of tongues, is to edify, comfort, encourage, give direction, and or warn the hearers. Acts 2:1–8, where the Holy Spirit interpreted the tongue before it reached the ears of the hearers, is an example of this gift in the Bible. 1 Corinthians 14:27–28 gives instructions for this gift. People with this gift:

- Have learned to hear the Holy Spirit and follow His leading
- Are in tune with the overall flow of the meeting
- Have a submitted attitude and serve in relationship with the church
- Usually have or desire to have a strong foundation in Bible knowledge
- Often know the speaker's message before it is preached

Leadership

The gift of leadership is the God-given special endowment to serve, strengthen, and build up the body of Christ and others by God-given vision, not only knowing where to go and what to do, but also, the ability to impart this vision to others in such a way that they will follow. Leaders lead others into closer relationship with the Lord, and wise leaders teach dependence upon the leading of the Holy Spirit. The best leader is His follower. 1 Corinthians 11:1 and the life of King David provides insight for this gift. People with this gift:

- First are to be good followers of the Holy Spirit
- Are usually in leadership roles in their church, community, and or business
- Are able to associate biblical principles into everyday life
- Can be mistaken for over confident
- Often operate in the gift of faith
- Are visionary

- Usually see into the spirit realm
- Are Kingdom builders

Mercy The gift of mercy is the God-given special endowment to serve, strengthen, and build up the body of Christ and others by providing necessities for the poor or those in need by attending to their condition through the Holy Spirit's enablement. This gift often works in conjunction with other gifts as giving, helps, and healing. An example of this gift is found in Acts 9:36; Tabitha was full of good works and charitable deeds (derived from "eleos," mercy). People with this gift:

- Have a heart which reaches out to those in need with acts of service and cheerfulness
- Use their abilities in service to the needy
- See beyond the natural through words of knowledge
- Are graced with God-given empathy
- Often reach those who are forgotten by others

Miracles The gift of miracles is the God-given special endowment to serve, strengthen, and build up the body of Christ and others by performing miracles through the power of the Holy Spirit. These miracles will always point back to Jesus Christ as Lord, and will bring glory to God and His power. John 2:1–11 and John 6:16–21 are examples of this gift. People with this gift:

- Will do what they hear and see the Holy Spirit saying and doing
- Give glory to Jesus
- Usually have a strong evangelism gift
- Often also have the gift of healing
- Often have hardships due to God's "thorn in the flesh" to keep them humble (2 Corinthians 12:7)
- Look to God for answers for the impossible

Missionary The gift of missionary is the God-given special endowment to serve, strengthen, and build up the body of Christ and others by living a life of taking the Gospel to the unreached, whether at home or abroad. This gift differs from the Evangelist, in that the Evangelist is a governmental gift given to the church for building it up, and the missionary is a gift given to a person to reach others for Christ. Paul said in Romans 15:20, "It has always been my ambition to preach the gospel where Christ was not known, so that I would not be building on someone else's foundation." Romans 15:20 is the heart of a missionary, not that they will always go where Christ has not been preached, but rather where people have not yet been reached. People with this gift:

- Live their life to reach others for Christ
- Often live sacrificially
- May live overseas
- Often have a gift of faith
- Usually pick an occupation which coincides with a need on the missionary field

Prophecy

Prophecy is the God-given special endowment to serve, strengthen, and build up the body of Christ and others by speaking foretelling and forth telling timely words from God while under the anointing of the Holy Spirit. Prophecy is a *flowing in* from the Holy Spirit and a *flowing out* of a person. 2 Peter 1:21 defines this for us, "For prophecy never had its origin in the will of man, but men spoke from God as they were carried along by the Holy Spirit." This gift can manifest in conversations, preaching, prophesying, singing, and even letter writing. Acts 21:10–11, John 11:49–52, and 1 Tim 4:1 are examples of prophecy in the New Testament, demonstrating the purpose of this gift, which is to edify, exhort, comfort, give direction, and or warn the hearers. People with this gift:

- Have learned to hear the Holy Spirit and follow His leading
- Often have the gift of interpretation of tongues
- Are in tune with the overall flow of the Holy Spirit in meetings or situations
- Have a submitted attitude and serve in relationship with the church
- Usually have or desire to have a strong foundation in Bible knowledge
- Often know the speaker's message before it is preached

Service

The gift of service is the God-given special endowment to serve, strengthen, and build up the body of Christ and others by devoted, Holy Spirit inspired, service to others' needs. This is both a gift and the out flowing fruit of this gift. The word, directly related to deacon, Paul's ministry, and our ministry as believers to the lost. This gift produces an out flowing fruit when motivated by the Holy Spirit, while serving. People with this gift:

- Are devoted to serving the church and her ministers
- Are others' needs centered
- Are people of maturity of character
- Often have the title Deacon
- Often are in full time ministry
- See temporal services as spiritual and beneficial to the Kingdom of God
- Have God-given ability to see needs others miss
- Are gifted in serving the 5-fold, produced by a deep inner working of the Holy Spirit

Tongues

The gift of tongues is the God-given special endowment to serve, strengthen, and build up the body of Christ and others by speaking in various languages unknown by the speaker, whether of men or angles. An example of this gift in action found in Acts 2:1–8, and reveals God Himself interpreted the tongue before it reached the ears of the hearers. 1 Corinthians 14:27–28 provides instruction for this gift. This public use of tongues is always precedes an interpretation of the tongue, in order that hears may be edified, comforted, encouraged, given direction, and or warned. The gift of tongues is not the same gift as is given to all who receive the baptism in the Holy Spirit with the evidence of speaking in tongues; one is for the edification of others and necessitates interpretation, and the other is a private prayer language for personal edification. People with this gift:

- Have the prayer language of tongues
- Often speak in various tongues while in prayer

- Often also have the gift of prophecy and interpretation of tongues
- Feel or sense a bubbling up from their spirit when they have a tongue to share publicly
- Are able to keep quiet if there is not an interpreter present
- May or may not know the theme of the interpretation of their tongue

Word of Knowledge

The word of knowledge is God-given special endowment to serve, strengthen, and build up the body of Christ and others by Holy Spirit revealed, unlearned knowledge. The word of knowledge often precedes another gift or manifestation of the Holy Spirit. The Bible frequently connects this gift to healing and evangelism. While prophecy described best as "a pouring in and flowing out," the word of knowledge is analogous to "describing a glass of water." How to communicate the word of knowledge takes wisdom and carefulness. John 1:45–51, Mark 11:2–6, and Acts 5:1–14 are examples of this gift in use. People with this gift:

- May feel a sensation or pain in their own bodies corresponding with the part of the body in another, which needs healing
- May see Holy Spirit prompted pictures or movies openly or in their mind
- Will suddenly have unlearned knowledge about the thoughts or needs of others
- Are good listeners to the Holy Spirit
- Usually have a disciplined mind and thought life

Word of Wisdom

The gift of the word of wisdom is the God-given special endowment to serve, strengthen, and build up the body of Christ and others by supernaturally having God's wisdom in a given circumstance. This Holy Spirit given wisdom manifests in giving the right application of knowledge and clarity in counseling sessions, meetings, families, and anywhere wisdom is needed. An example of this gift is in 1 Kings 3 where Solomon, through God's wisdom, was able to discern who the true mother was. John 8:33 is the antithesis to this gift. The word of wisdom frequently comes through dreams. Leaders often have this gift. Examples of this gift are found in Mt 2:12, John 8:3–11, Acts 16:6–8, and Acts 27:30–35. People with this gift:

- Have a strong reliance on God for direction and wisdom
- Often have a strong desire to counsel
- Are sought after by others for advice
- Are known for making wise decisions which cut through natural decision making
- Often tie their God-given wisdom to Scriptures

Martyrdom and Voluntary Poverty

Some people add martyrdom and voluntary poverty to their list of spiritual gifts, but there are controversies as to whether or not these two are gifts or are only evidences of other gifts. For example, voluntary poverty may be the result of missionary or a closely related gift; and martyrdom is probably a result of circumstances and the gift of faith. Note *voluntary poverty* is not due to unwise choices; rather it is a choice to live with less so others may have more.

Appendix A

• •

A Truth in Tension: Demons and Christians— What are the Limits?

APPENDIX A IS AN EXCERPT FROM *CONFRONTING THE WIND*, a treatise written after an extensive study on three subjects entitled *Demons and Christians—What are the Limits, General Curses—The Tongue's Power*, and *Generational Curses—Who is the Author and Why?*

A friend ("Fred," name changed), whom my husband and I had known for years, came by for a visit one night. We discussed demons, their activity, and authority in a believer's life with Fred many times. Fred believed demons locate inside Christians, and he discipled others according to his views. Fred knew both my husband and I disagreed with him regarding demons dwelling inside Christians. This night in particular he was more aggressive than usual. After about 30 minutes discussing demons, I had a spirit grab my throat and heard a voice demand with great assertion I let it out. I felt an intense urgency and compulsion to do what it insisted. Instead, I did nothing. Baffled at the experience, I asked God to give me understanding as to what had happened, since I believed and still do believe, the Bible teaches the Holy Spirit does not allow demons inside of Christians. Later, I discussed my experience with my husband, who immediately responded with, "Oh, so demons hang around Fred to promote his doctrine, interesting." Immediately I understood the demon was trying to persuade me it was inside of me, and since it was inside of me, I needed to get it out. (This of course was a lie, but then what can we expect from a demon?) If had I had given into its lie and tried to "get it out," I am convinced the demon would have manifested in support of its lie, though this is only speculation. Fred was promoting a doctrine of demons and they hung around him to help promote it. If the demon had really been inside me, would it have demanded I let it out? The Bible teaches demons want instead to inhabit people, so why did this one demand I let it out? It was all a big lie. The demon wanted to convince me (by experience) it was in me, so I would believe its lie. I wonder how many so-called "deliverance" sessions, are nothing more than lying deceiving spirits promoting their doctrines to those who will believe them. The Bible is objective; our experiences are subjective. We must believe the word of God, build our doctrines based upon what it says, and then evaluate our experiences according to the Bible.

A Truth in Tension

• •

Demons and Christians—What are the Limits?

A truth in tension is an apparent contradiction in scripture, carefully deciphered in order to find the treasure of truth lying in the balance. A single clear example of whether a demon can dwell inside a believer's body, soul, or spirit, does not exist in the New Testament. All doctrinal positions, therefore, must be from the weight of clear principles, which are in scripture and scrupulously studied through sound exegesis. Appendix A is a section from *Confronting the Wind:* Demons and Christians—What are the Limits? A Truth in Tension.

1 John 5:18, 2 Corinthians 12:7-10, and Luke 22:31-32 are a truth held in tension. Exclusively studied for this section is the NASB. All definitions are from the Greek Lexicon.

1. 1 John 5:18—the wicked one does not touch him
"We know that no one who is born of God sins; but He who was born of God keeps him, and the evil one does not touch him."

- Keeps: 1) to attend to carefully, take care of 1a) to guard 1b) metaph. to keep, one in the state in which he is 1c) to observe 1d) to reserve: to undergo something
- Touch: 1) to fasten to, adhere to 1a) to fasten fire to a thing, kindle, set of fire

2. 2 Corinthians 12:7–10 Paul's thorn in the flesh
"Because of the surpassing greatness of the revelations, for this reason, to keep me from exalting myself, there was given me a thorn in the flesh, a messenger of Satan to torment me—to keep me from exalting myself! Concerning this I implored the Lord three times that it might leave me. And He has said to me, "My grace is sufficient for you, for power is perfected in weakness." Most gladly, therefore, I will rather boast about my weaknesses, so that the power of Christ may dwell in me. Therefore I am well content with weaknesses, with insults, with distresses, with persecutions, with difficulties, for Christ's sake; for when I am weak, then I am strong."

- Thorn: a pointed piece of wood, a pale, a stake, 2) a sharp stake, splinter
- Messenger : a messenger, envoy, one who is sent, an angel, a messenger from God
- Buffet: to strike with the fist, give one a blow with the fist, 2) to maltreat, treat with violence and contumely

3. Luke 22:31–32, fruit produced by sifting:
"Simon, Simon, behold, Satan has demanded permission to sift you like wheat; but I have prayed for you, that your faith may not fail; and you, when once you have turned again, strengthen your brothers," Definitions of "sift" and "returned":

- Sift: 1) to sift, shake in a sieve, 2) fig. by inward agitation to try one's faith to the verge of overthrow
- Returned: 1) transitively 1a) to turn to, 1a1) to the worship of the true God, 1b) to cause to return, to bring back, 1b1) to the love and obedience of God, 1b2) to the love for the children, 1b3) to love wisdom and righteousness, 2) intransitively, 2a) to turn to one's self, 2b) to turn one's self about, turn back, 2c) to return, turn back, come back

This is the tension: understood from 1 John 5:18, if someone keeps themselves, then the wicked one cannot touch him. Furthermore, James states, "But He gives a greater grace. Therefore it says, 'God is opposed to the proud, but gives grace to the humble.' Submit therefore to God. Resist the devil and he will flee from you." (James 4:6–7) However, what if someone does not keep himself, live humbly, submit to God, or resist the devil? Does this give the enemy a license to touch, adhere to, cling to, or fasten to us? Does this mean we have to be perfect in order to keep ourselves?

The Bible says, "The sum of Your word is truth, And every one of Your righteous ordinances is everlasting." (Psalm 119:160) We must, therefore study the entirety of scripture to accurately exegete this subject. Two tension scriptures to the above are:

- "Not that I have already obtained it or have already become perfect, but I press on so that I may lay hold of that for which also I was laid hold of by Christ Jesus." (Philippians 3:12)
- "...because David did what was right in the sight of the Lord, and had not turned aside from anything that He commanded him all the days of his life, except in the case of Uriah the Hittite." (1 Kings 15:5)

Paul, in Philippians 3, had not yet apprehended what he was aiming for, though he walked where he had attained. God said David did what was right in the eyes of the Lord except when he murdered Uriah. However, David made many mistakes, numbering the troops for example. Remember, God views immaturity vastly different from rebellion. It is not a matter of perfection, but rather a matter of walking where we have attained, and, when we sin, repenting. Our responsibility is to be found in Him, and to the best of our ability, relying on the grace of God, not trusting our own righteousness, walking where we have attained, having faith in God, and His protection. We through faith quench all the fiery darts of the wicked one. God will protect us no matter how immature we are (Psalm 91).

If we start to backslide, God will begin to oppose us. What does it mean for God to oppose (to range in battle against, to oppose one's self, resist) someone? God may take us through a dry season (Hosea 2:14), or some other form of discipline. Hebrews 12 explains discipline from God. God has His many tools to use behind His spiritual woodshed, one of which is the devil. Yes, for a believer, the devil is a tethered tool in the hand of God. ("Among these are Hymenaeus and Alexander, whom I have handed over to Satan, so that they will be taught not to blaspheme." 1 Timothy 1:20) In the life of Job, (though the affliction he endured was not a discipline, but a trial) the devil was on God's very tight leash, having to ask God for permission in everything. God gave Satan restricted access to Job.

Two New Testament examples where God granted devil-restricted access are Paul's thorn in his flesh and the sifting Peter went through, both leading up to and during the crucifixion of Jesus Christ.

Paul says God allowed the thorn in his flesh because of the abundance of revelation God had given to him. The thorn was in his flesh. This word "flesh" is the same word used in Romans 7:18, "For I know that in me (that is, in my flesh) nothing good dwells." The thorn was not in Paul's soul or spirit, but in his flesh. God allowed the messenger to buffet (refer to definition) Paul, a restriction of outer influence affecting the inner man. For example, when someone hits us, the blow came from the outside, but has an impact on the inside, as well. Was the hit from the inside? No, it came from the outside. Similarly, an external blow to our body has internal bleeding, which results in a bruise. God allowed the thorn, and the thorn benefitted Paul. He would be better off with the thorn, than to live without it in pride. The purpose of the thorn, the messenger of Satan, was to keep Paul's character in check. Thus, the Lord uses the devil much like a sheep dog, keeping sheep. Here again, the messenger of Satan was only a tool in the hand of God, allowed for the benefit of the child of God.

Peter's sifting is another example where God uses the devil as His tool to accomplish His plans and His purposes. Jesus told Peter Satan had asked permission to sift him. Jesus implies He gave Satan permission, since Jesus then says He prayed for Peter, that his faith would not fail. Furthermore, Jesus then prophesies to Peter explaining when the sifting would take place; he would deny Jesus that very day, and then the rooster would crow three times.

Allow me to paraphrase these events. "Simon, Satan has asked, and I have given him permission to agitate you and try to ruin your faith. Simon, he wants to take you to the verge of overthrow. It will be a hard time for you; in fact, you will even disown Me three times. After you deny Me the third time, a rooster will crow. When this happens, remember I already knew it would. It does not change the fact that I love you and have plans for you, a future, and a hope. I know all will desert Me, and I know it must happen to fulfill the prophecies. Peter, it will be a dark time for you, but in the end, when the sifting is over, you will be stronger for having gone through this. You will be a leader in My Kingdom. Peter, when you turn about and return to Me, go strengthen your brothers who have not yet understood all this. I will use this for good. The devil intends it for evil, but he is only a tool in My hand. I will use his work to accomplish My purposes."

Jesus' betrayal by Judas with 30 pieces of silver and His crucifixion are two other examples where God used Satan to accomplish His eternal purposes. (Jeremiah 32:6–9 and Matthew 27:3–10). God used the devil to fulfill prophecy when he incited Judas. Then, the most prevalent in God's eternal purposes, when He used the devil to crucify His Son, knowing that death would never hold Him; He swallowed death up in victory when he arose, bringing salvation to all who would receive Him.

To summarize, can the devil touch us? No, if we are walking with God. Yes, if we are not, but only if God permits. Additionally, yes, if God allows, for our benefit. However, the devil's leash is short and it is always under constant surveillance and handling by God.

Fretting over the past or worrying about the future confuses the present and creates a fog, which obscures God's sovereignty from view.

God's word is true.
"And we know that God causes all things to work together for good to those who love God, to those who are called according to His purpose. For those whom He foreknew, He also predestined to become conformed to the image of His Son..."
(Romans 8:28-29a NAS)

God is for us, who then, can be against us and prevail! "He who did not spare His own Son, but delivered Him over for us all, how will He not also with Him freely give us all things?"
(Romans 8:32 NAS)

Past regrets and tomorrow's worries become boulders on our highway. Have faith in God! He is more than able to make all things work for good!

God love us!

Notes

· ·

"Call to me and I will answer you and tell you great and unsearchable things you do not know."
Jeremiah 33:3

CPSIA information can be obtained
at www.ICGtesting.com
Printed in the USA
BVHW021843070323
659902BV00013B/387